P9-AGU-514

Jean Ray Laury

The Fabric STAMPING HANDBOOK

- **Fun Projects**
- **Tips & Tricks**
- **Unlimited Possibilities**

C&T PUBLISHING

©2002 Jean Ray Laury

Editor: Liz Aneloski

Technical Editors: Sara Kate MacFarland and Joyce Lytle

Copy Editor: Stacy Chamness

Cover Design and Production: Kristen Yenche

Book Designer and Design Director: Kristen Yenche

Production Assistant: Jeff Carrillo

Photographer: E. Z. Smith unless otherwise noted

Illustrator: Tim Manibusan

Published by C&T Publishing, Inc. P.O. Box 1456, Lafayette, California 94549

All rights reserved. No part of this work covered by the copyright hereon may be reproduced or used in any form or by any means—graphic, electronic, or mechanical, including photocopying, recording, taping, or information storage and retrieval systems—without written permission of the publisher. The copyrights on individual artworks are retained by the artists as noted in *The Fabric Stamping Handbook*.

Exception: The author and publisher give permission to photocopy a maximum of two copies each of page 79, 85, and 89 for personal use only.

Attention Teachers:
C&T Publishing, Inc. encourages you to use this book as a text for teaching. Contact us at 800-284-1114 or www.ctpub.com for more information about the C&T Teachers Program.

We take great care to ensure that the information included in this book is accurate and presented in good faith, but no warranty is provided nor results guaranteed. Since we have no control over the choice of materials or procedures used, neither the author nor C&T Publishing, Inc. shall have any liability to any person or entity with respect to any loss or damage caused directly or indirectly by the information contained in this book.

Trademarked (™) and Registered Trademarked (®) names are used throughout this book. Rather than use the symbols with every occurrence of a trademark and registered trademark name, we are using the names only in an editorial fashion and to the benefit of the owner, with no intention of infringement.

Library of Congress Cataloging-in-Publication Data
Laury, Jean Ray.

  The fabric stamping handbook : fun projects, tips & tricks, unlimited possibilities / Jean Ray Laury.
      p. cm.
Includes bibliographical references and index.
  ISBN 1-57120-130-0 (paper trade)
1. Textile printing. I. Title.
  TT852 .L36 2002
  746.6'2—dc21

                                      2001005407

Printed in China
10 9 8 7 6 5 4 3 2 1

CONTENTS

ACKNOWLEDGMENTS

The artists whose works appear in this book have generously shared their abundant talents and expertise with those of us just beginning to explore stamping. They have worked, played, and experimented, and the remarkable results of their efforts are shown here to inspire us all.

My warmest thanks to all the artists for their humor, patience, and generosity; and for entrusting me with their wonderful work. Some of the stamped letters and packages that brightened the mailman's day (and mine) indicated that stamping has been absorbed into every aspect of their lives.

To Susan Smeltzer, an intrepid and good-humored wizard on both the computer and the sewing machine, a heartfelt thanks. And to Lizabeth Laury for her spirited and skillful help. Frank Laury kept our energies high on coffee and masterminded the kitchen (once I was tied to my desk).

Thanks to my editor, Liz Aneloski for her attentive support and perceptive help; to all the wonderful C&T staff who gave me the opportunity to explore fabric stamping and to share it with you; and to Kristen Yenche for her design expertise.

All photographs in this book are by E.Z. Smith unless otherwise noted.

Pots and Cups, 43½" x 42½", Nancy Taylor

Using ½" thick white Speedy Cut™ Printing blocks and Speedball® carving tools (mostly V-1 and V-2), Nancy made ten stamps, including teapots, teacups, steam, spoons, sugar cubes, stars and checkerboard. To create variety, she masked (pages 31-33) parts of some stamps to combine images (to put a spoon in a cup) and she blended the paint from one color to another.

HOW TO USE THIS BOOK

Reference Charts

Two charts are provided to give you a wealth of information. The Materials Chart (page 19) lists various materials from which stamps can be made and offers all the details you will need to make an informed decision. The Paints Chart (pages 22-23) condenses information on paints and dyes.

Paints, dyes, carving blocks, and similar products listed in the charts are those generally available and widely used by stampers. The lists do not include every brand, but they will familiarize you with most of the characteristics and qualities you will be looking for in these products. The products in each chart are followed by a number, which refers to the Source List.

Source List

This list (page 92) includes the sources for products you may need, giving websites and toll-free numbers.

Stamps Used by Artists

Stamps used are identified, with only a few exceptions. There were vintage alphabets with no identification and a few stamps have been lost or were not identifiable. Each stamp and the company that makes it is listed with the piece in which it was used. Addresses and websites of the rubber stamp companies appear on pages 93-94.

Publications

The list of books and magazines dealing strictly with fabric stamping is short, but instructive information can be found in all stamping publications. Stamp magazines are peppered with ads for companies new and old, including many of special interest. Our list includes several which you'll find most helpful. Stamp stores are a wonderful resource; most carry an extensive array of periodicals, stamps, and related products.

Projects

Six projects at the end of this book offer specific directions and patterns. If you've never stamped before, select one that appeals to you and appears to suit your skill level and you will soon be familiar with all the basics. These projects cover handmade and commercial stamps, as well as a range of simple to complex processes.

INTRODUCTION

Ancestral Spirits, 17" x 17",
Elaine Plogman

Elaine designs and carves all of her own stamps on 3" synthetic blocks, and stamps with Deka, Permanent Fabric Paint, PROfab Textile Ink (transparent), and Jacquard Textile Color. There are often subtle transformations where she prints light on dark, then dark on light. Design of the corner block is by Robert Plogman.

Tutankhamen stamped the messages from his royal palace. Hammurabi identified his edicts with a personal stamp. Every country, king, ruler, local magistrate, or emperor has (or had) his or her own official seal. Since early communication by means of clay tablets, seals have been stamped into moist clay to make the official impression. Later, stamps were pressed into melted wax to seal official documents, a practice that continued through Victorian times when personal letters were sealed by the same method.

For rubber stamping now we use cast rubber, laser-cut plastics, and molded foams. Tens of thousands of ready-made stamps are available to us in stamp stores and by mail order. Dozens of materials can be purchased from which to make your own stamps.

Fabric artists are particularly inventive when it comes to making their own stamps, using everything from weatherstripping and rubber erasers to sticky-back floor tiles. Their stamps range from potatoes to potato mashers and from carefully carved blocks to flyswatters. Their creative skills are evident in their stunning works.

The distinction between stamps and block prints is a blurry one. Where one leaves off and the other begins is not obvious. Size seems irrelevant—you could use a manhole cover as a stamp, providing you could lift it. Nor is technique a determining factor; the brayer (page 24) used to ink a small stamp might also be used on a large linoleum block. Many of the same tools, materials, and paints are used for both. So what is the difference?

The criterion I used is this: if the cut or carved image can be inked and stamped to cloth without a press or other mechanical means, then it is a stamp. This works for me, though there is certainly ample space for crossover. Our purpose here is to put our images onto fabric and get on with the fun.

COPYRIGHT

Most commercial stamps are copyrighted and copyright law governs their use. You are free to use those stamps for personal work, for gifts, and for individual projects. Copyright limits only your commercial use of a stamp. You cannot reproduce a copyrighted stamp design in multiples or for sale without violating copyright laws.

There are "angel" companies that produce copyright-free designs. These stamps bear no copyright symbol, and are referred to as "angel" stamps. Many of these are old images that came from work in the public domain. A single design may therefore be available from more than one company. Angel companies are posted on a website given on page 93 in our list of rubber stamp companies.

Most copyright issues revolve around those stamps that are artist-designed. Stamp companies have in-house designers or freelance artists who produce works exclusively for them. It is typical for companies to have both copyrighted and angel designs. However, each company has its own policy regarding use, so always check with the manufacturer or their catalog for this information. Any limitations are there to protect the artist. It's important to understand and abide by the laws that govern fair use.

If you plan to sell a piece of work containing commercial stamp images, it is your responsibility to check with the manufacturing company before selling the work. (It's even better to know this before using the image.) Some companies allow you to hand produce and sell the image up to ten times, while others allow sale of a piece containing their stamps only if credit or permission is given. Still others allow no sales.

Write or email the manufacturer, explain your interest, and ask permission for a "one time use." Or ask to see their copyright policies. In most cases, if your request meets their approval, they'll give permission.

Some artists buy only copyright-free stamps, wanting the flexibility to make any use of the stamp in the future. Others make their own stamps, in part to be free of any copyright concerns. Never disregard copyright assuming that it is unimportant. It is important to the manufacturer or owner, as well as to the artist and, should you ever copyright a design of your own, it will be equally important to you. You can copyright the stamps you design yourself, whether you carve them or have them custom made. The copyright laws will then protect you in the same way.

STAMPS

CHAPTER 1

Details of *Mirage*, Ingrid Law

Ingrid drew the face using a strip of ½"-wide sticky-back weatherstripping on Plexiglas®. After stamping the masks onto cotton fabric with Folk Art Acrylic, she stamped red spirals and yellow sun shapes, overlapping the stamped masks. Decorative metallic paints, along with bells, buttons, machine quilting, and embroidery embellish the work. Floating squares are satin stitched with gold metallic thread.

Stamping is the most simple, versatile, and accessible of all surface design methods. It can be as expensive (or inexpensive) as you need it to be. Commercial stamps and tools simplify the process, but results are equally exciting with found objects and handmade stamps. The possibilities are limited only by your imagination.

PARTS OF A STAMP

Stamps generally consist of three parts: the design (the carved image or die), a pad or cushion, and a base. A handle is often added, though in some stamps these parts are combined. A design cut from thick foam (weatherstripping, for instance) needs no additional cushioning—the die and cushion are one. It does need a base. A carved art gum eraser, one-inch thick, might require neither a cushion nor a base; it can be easily grasped and is self-cushioning. Some carving blocks have adequate cushioning to be used as they are without mounting. A carved pencil eraser has a built in handle, consisting of the pencil itself. Most commercial stamps, however, consist of those three parts or some variation of them.

IMAGE OR DIE

The die or stamp image can be any of a variety of materials. Rubber is traditional, and it is still considered among the best, along with those made of flexible plastics. Commercial images are cast of vulcanized rubber or are laser cut into flexible synthetic materials. Designers will print using any kind of image, from a potato masher to a block of wood. Anything that will hold ink and retain its shape can be used as the image. A carved white eraser block has the die (or design) cut into a block that adds both cushion and handle, and it is easily stored. Many stampers prefer unmounted stamps. Their flexibility makes them easy to handle, simple to clean, and excellent for stamping onto curved surfaces. Unmounted stamps are considerably less expensive than mounted ones, and can easily be glued to a cushion or base.

A commercial company can turn your original drawings into stamps. Most companies that make custom stamps will ask for black-and-white line work—that means that your drawing in black ink lines must be final and ready for reproduction. Some companies work only with letters that are set with type, but many also make images. Check with printers and rubber stamp makers in your Yellow Pages, as well as ads in stamp magazines.

CUSHION

The cushion allows give and flexibility so that pressure added during stamping helps assure a good print. It usually consists of a foam pad about 1/8" to 1/4" thick, located between the image (or die) and the base. Erasers, foam, and sponge are self-cushioned. In some foam alphabet blocks, for example, the foam is deep enough to serve as die, cushion, and handle all in one.

BASE AND HANDLE

The traditional office stamp has a wood base and handle. Stamps mounted on a clear acrylic or Plexiglas base allow you to see through them for more precise placement. And clear plastic boxes are great for mounting innertube or rubber cutouts and foam sheets. But the most common base for commercial stamps is still wood.

For bases you can't see through, select stamps that have the image aligned at one edge to help in positioning. Contoured mounts help greatly in positioning the images.

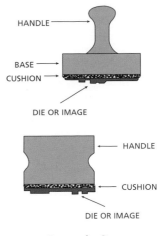

Parts of a Stamp

COMMERCIAL STAMPS

Ready-made stamps are available almost everywhere: in stamp stores, mail-order catalogs, craft and hobby shops, stationers, gift shops, and the internet. Even drug stores, discount stores, and airport gift shops get in on the act. As you become familiar with them, you will find that each stamp company has its own particular style or type of image. Cartoons, words, animals, people, and plants—you name it and there will be a stamp of it.

When buying a stamp, look for these things:
- a sharp-edged design that is cleanly cut
- an easily-grasped handle or base
- an identification—a print on the side (if there is a handle) or a print on the top of the wood base to show the image, as well as which way is up.

If the base is Plexiglas, or is shaped to fit the image (like CHUNKY STAMPS), identification is pretty obvious and alignment (page 35) will be simplified. If the base is wood or some other opaque material, make sure the image is aligned with one edge of the base to help in positioning.

There are various roller stamps available for printing continuous patterns. For large-scale designs, wallpaper rollers are very durable and perform as well on fabric as on walls or paper. Smaller roller stamps are also available with patterns designed for repeat: Faux-finish brayers (sponge), Fiskars® brayers (synthetic rubber), and Rollagraph® (foam) all work this way. You can apply adhesive-backed weatherstripping onto a short length of PVC pipe for a handmade roller stamp. A dowel will provide a handle for printing a continuous roll. Any brayer can be prepared by adhering designs to its roller.

Flexi-Cut square mounted on Plexiglas square.

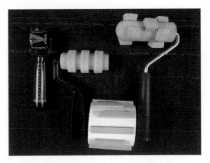

Roller tools, from left; letters glued to a purchased wallpaper-finishing roller; patterned foam roller; adhesive strips on a PVC pipe; and weatherstripping applied in squares to a foam roller.

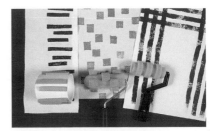

Prints from roller tools

Trade Off, 13½" x 18", Sandra Sider

Using a foam brush to apply Createx® multi-surface acrylic pearl paint to her wallpaper stamping tool, Sandra stamped onto red and green cotton fabrics. Blue areas of the panel are cyanotype photograms (blueprints) on turquoise fabric. The edges of foam brushes were used to stamp lines.

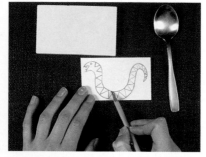

Drawn lines made with a #1 or 2B soft lead pencil are ready for transfer to carving block.

Drawing placed face down on carving block and burnished with spoon.

As paper is removed, the drawing can be seen transferred to the carving block.

HANDMADE STAMPS

A really satisfying aspect of stamping comes in making your own stamps; you can introduce the images you want at the scale you choose. Dozens of materials are available for cutting or carving. Each has its own character and must be handled differently. Many fiber artists make large and bold stamps that don't lose detail on textured fabrics. Carving their own stamps gives them exactly the design they want at a low cost.

The most common tools for carving stamps include X-Acto® knives, craft knives, linoleum cutting tools, and scissors. Good, sharp tools will ease the work. Fabric artists use both commercial and handmade stamps, but all agree that making stamps is half the fun—a way of adding unique and personal details. Self-adhesive or stick-on backings simplify the mounting, and permanent fabric paints assure washability.

TRANSFERRING A PATTERN

Most designs for your stamps will develop from drawings that need to be transferred to your block. Remember when transferring your design that you must reverse the image so that it will read correctly when stamped. With a leaf or a flower, it may not matter. With numbers or letters, it is crucial. Choose one of the stamp materials on page 19, and use one of the transfer methods that follow.

Pencil

Draw your design on tracing paper as you wish it to appear on fabric. Go over it with a firm line using a soft lead pencil. Then turn it face down (which makes the reversal) so the pencil line is face to face with the stamp surface. Burnish (rub) over the pencil lines with a spoon or similar object to transfer the design. Go over the lines with a permanent ink pen (non-permanent ink will later transfer with any water-base paint and ruin your design). Avoid cutting into the rubber with the pen. You are now ready to carve the block.

Laser Printer

Any print-out from a laser printer can be transferred to a carving block. Place the laser print with the toner side down on the block and press with a warm iron. Do not reverse the image. It will reverse itself when you place it face down on the block. The image will transfer clearly enough to serve as a guide for carving.

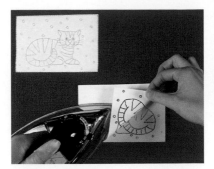

Laser image will transfer to carving block with warm iron.

Photocopy Machine

A copied image can be transferred the same way as the laser printed image, though I never get as clear a result. Kata Patton transfers from photocopier to carving block by placing the toner side down and then burnishing with her fingernail.

STAMP MATERIALS

Art Gum Erasers

This inexpensive and convenient stamp material comes in either one-inch cubes or one inch by two inch rectangles. They are available as gum erasers or art gum erasers and under various brand names. The cubes, just as they arrive from the store, are perfect for checkerboards. And the ease with which they can be cut makes them especially desirable. You will want dozens of art gum stamps: circles, triangles, squares, hearts, stars. All simple and geometric shapes are wonderful to use and easy to cut. The art gum eraser offers the image or die, the cushion, and the base all in one. A second image can be cut on the reverse face of the eraser.

A V-shaped carving tool speeds up and simplifies the removal of excess areas and adds textural lines.

To cut the eraser, use an X-Acto knife with a sharp, tapered blade. Or use a single-edge razor blade if you are cutting only straight lines. Avoid fine lines and keep the shapes simple for your first stamp. Always cut away from your fingers—never toward them. You'll develop skill with practice.

George L. Thomson, in his *Rubber Stamps and How to Make Them* (Pantheon, 1982) suggests using a fine needle to outline the design of a stamp. If these straight up-and-down insertions are close together, they allow for a very detailed edge. Always cut the eraser at a slight angle to add extra strength to the design area.

Art gum eraser stamps and prints made from them

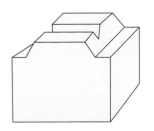

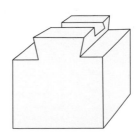

Edges that are angled out are well supported.

Undercut edges lack support.

Always cut away from your fingers— never toward them.

Darice® Foamies, Flexi-Foam®, PenScore, Staedtler Mars Plastic Eraser, Speedy-Cut Printing Block, Magic-Rub, Pink Pearl, Artgum®

Hard Rubber or Plastic Erasers

Pink Pearl®, Staedtler®, and Magic-Rub® are among the erasers used for stamps. Sharp-cornered edges are more adaptable than round edges. Springy or elastic erasers will be more difficult to cut than those that are firm. Look for rectangles in a size closest to what you want for the finished stamp.

A V-shaped linoleum-cutting gouge (tool) helps to remove large areas of background. If the design is aligned with a corner of the stamp, registration (alignment of the design) is simplified. The carved stamp can be used just as it is, or a wood-block base can be added.

Detail of *Turtle Moon,* Kim Jagger

Using a 7" x 8" rubber-like white carving block, Kim carved these turtles, one on each side of the block. She used V-shaped linoleum cutting tools and stamped with Versatex on hand-painted, dyed, and plain muslin. Each stamped turtle was cut out, appliquéd to black fabric, then trimmed to leave a narrow outline that was stitched to the backing with metallic thread.

Stamp Blocks

Blocks made specifically for carving are firm, and can readily be cut with linoleum carving tools or X-Acto knives. Speedy-Cut Blocks, if hardened slightly, will have less give and will be easier to carve. Place one in a refrigerator or freezer or rub an ice cube over the surface to chill it before starting. Among the many available blocks are Speedy-Cut, E-Z Cut Blocks, Safety-Kut™, and Soft-Kut.

Pencil Eraser Stamps

Pick up any pencil with its little cylindrical eraser and you have a great stamp. Gently tamp it onto an inked pad, press it on fabric, and it's a polka dot. Carefully slice the eraser with an X-Acto knife and you can create a half-circle, square, star or hexagon—anything you can carve. Stars or asterisks require a bit more skill in cutting. Use different sizes of pencil erasers to vary the dots.

Innertube Stamps

An old innertube will provide enough rubber for dozens of stamps. Wash the innertube in detergent and warm water; then cut out the usable parts, avoiding the small ridges; and store flat. It can be cut with scissors, and then applied to a block of wood with rubber cement. Many innertube stamps were used on Susan R. Macy's jacket (page 53). The discharge (pages 46-47) quilt below was also made from innertube stamps. Small sheets of rubber, now available at stamp shows, are easier to handle than innertubes and are clean when you get them!

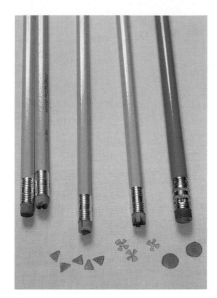

Carved pencil erasers

Sticks and Stones, 28" x 24", Jean Ray Laury

Stamps for this quilt, cut with scissors from a tire innertube, were glued to a wood block using rubber cement. Each stamp was then brush coated with Soft Scrub (containing bleach) and stamped onto navy cotton flannel. When discharged, the fabric squares were rinsed in a stop-agent. A second stamp was used for the sashing and border strips. Machine and hand quilted.

Weatherstripping on Plexiglas; pencil eraser apples

Top row— Art gum, innertube, and foam stamps

Bottom row—Innertube stamps

A child's alphabet block was pressed into heated PenScore.

Prints from Impressed PenScore.

Detail of *Dream a Little Dream II*, Dominie Nash

Heated PenScore was impressed with a small doll to create this negative-image stamp.

Foam

Some foams can be incised with a pencil or ballpoint pen for sharp lines and fine details. Both PenScore and Magic Stamp can be heated with a heat gun or hair dryer to make them soft and receptive. Objects pressed into the softened material will leave an impression that can be inked and then stamped. This produces a negative image. If you pressed an old-fashioned potato masher into the soft surface, you would impress a linear design. When inked and stamped the image would be reversed.

Another firm foam used in the same way is Soft Shapes™ Fun Puzzle, primarily used for children's bath toys and puzzles. Shapes can be stamped as they are or impressed. All three of these materials can be reheated, relaxed, and impressed again with a new image.

Other foam materials, like Darice Foamies, are available in thin sheets that can be easily cut with scissors. Thin ones will need to be mounted on a firm base, but when the image is cut, it has its own cushion. Computer mousepads will also serve as stamps and can be cut with scissors.

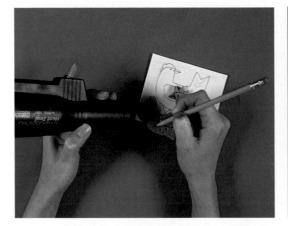

Drawing of a chicken was transferred to thin PenScore and cut out with scissors. After heating, details were impressed with a pencil.

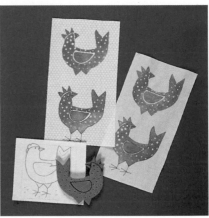

Drawing, stamp, and finished prints

Details were drawn on a PenScore block with a ballpoint pen, producing a negative, or reverse image.

Self-Adhesive Materials

Polyprint® Printing Plate, Flexible Printing Plate, and Flexi-Foam are all self-adhesive materials, a great aid for stamp makers. Floor tiles, with a peel-off backing, are harder to cut but work the same way. Sticky-backed weatherstripping is limited to strips in widths of 1/4" to 1 1/4" wide and a 4"-wide stripping available in auto supply stores.

Double-sided adhesive papers (available for mounting photographs) can be used to mount cut-out stamps that are not adhesive-backed. Simply peel off one protective paper and apply that exposed side to the back of the unmounted stamp. Trim the adhesive to the edge of the image. Then peel off the second protective paper and apply the stamp to wood, foam, or Plexiglas.

Small triangles of self-adhesive weatherstripping adhered to Plexiglas were stamped four at a time to fabric.

The flat bottom of a clear drinking glass provides a see-through base for this weatherstrip spiral. The glass makes a comfortable and convenient handle and weights the stamp for a good print.

A 5" tree stamp cut from self-adhesive weatherstripping is backed with Plexiglas for a see-through base.

Carol Olson cut this 8" heart from Flexi-Cut, mounted it on a double-sided adhesive cushion and adhered it to a sheet of Mylar®. The Mylar magically sticks to the Pyrex baking dish for stamping and can be peeled off for storage. Black lines on the Mylar assist in alignment.

FOUND STAMPS

Ink almost anything, press it to cloth, and you have a stamp. Muddy footprints tracked over the kitchen floor are a perfect example of a ready-made shoe stamp. Even a slice of bread covered with pomegranate jelly could serve as a stamp. Dropped upside-down on a smooth white tablecloth, it will readily transfer a red image of the bread slice. A strand of spaghetti makes a flexible stamp—coat with spaghetti sauce, arrange a spiral on your napkin and—voila! a print. Some fiber artists use strings this way. Glued to a base and inked with color, they can be stamped.

The kitchen or workshop is the first place to look for ready-made stamps. Maureen Bardusk uses flyswatters as stamps (at left), Lisa Gray Hollerbach put her kitchen whisk into service as a stamp in her *1995 Year of the Boar* (page 64). An old paint brush, with bristles splayed out to make a star shape, was found and used by Sandra Sider in *Stir Crazy* (page 52) and Rosemary Hoffenberg gave her potato masher a new look in *Solitude* (page 60).

Strainers, strawberry baskets, combs, and scraps of wood are among the myriad of objects used by fiber artists. Nothing in the home is safe from the marauding stamper.

Fabric Sample, Maureen Bardusk

For Maureen, flyswatters are stamps! We might visualize her madly swatting fabrics with artistic fervor, but she insists it is much more controlled than that. Using her collection of flyswatters, she inks the pattern area and presses it onto her fabric.

A child's block inked with a foam roller makes a great stamp, but it will read correctly only on the symmetrical letters. For TIMMY or MATT it works fine, but NICK's name would be mostly backward.

Half of a black walnut shell makes a symmetrical heart stamp. Because the shell is slightly uneven, printing on a soft padded surface is helpful. Elaine Plogman found this "stamp" in her neighborhood.

A carved-wood box was inked using a foam roller with Versatex paint. It gives a sharp, beautiful image. Carved-wood batik blocks from Indonesia or India, found in import shops, antique shops, and garage sales, along with the images printed from them.

VEGETABLE STAMPS

An entire category of ready-made stamps is waiting in your vegetable drawer. Any very firm vegetable, like carrots (for great polka dots of all sizes) or cabbage (cut crosswise) give delightful results. Juicier apples, oranges, or grapefruit will benefit by being left to dry for a day before printing. Save the root end of celery when you cut it; it makes a great cabbage rose. Potatoes, of course, are something everyone cut and stamped in third grade. They still work. Veggie stamps will keep well overnight in a resealable bag. If they dry or warp, trim off a narrow slice and start again.

NATURE PRINTS

Similar to the vegetable stamps are leaf stamps. A rich history of botanical prints tells us that the leaf printing process is well documented.

Leaves are universally available and always beautiful. In essence, a leaf is inked, placed face down on cloth, covered with a protective paper, and pressed with the fingers or rolled with a brayer (page 24). Flowers are printed in the same way.

Some leaves print more easily if they are first pressed in a book. Drying the leaves for even an hour or two will make them less limp and easier to handle. A leaf which has dried for weeks will be more rigid and also more fragile. Use an old phone book to press the leaves.

Apply paint to the under side (or veined side) of a leaf if you wish the vein pattern to predominate. For a flatter look, print the smooth top side.

Vegetables and their stamped images

Rose Pillow, 16" x 16", Juliana Alspaugh
A rose in full bloom was cut, inked, and laid face down on the fabric (without separating the petals). Juliana taps her dauber (page 24) into her printing ink, then onto each leaf or flower for stamping.

Leaves and flowers inked using sponge dauber, then pressed onto cloth.

At left, three leaves were inked on the under or veined side of the leaf, revealing a vein pattern. Leaves at right inked on top or smooth side.

Fish prints made using Versatex and cotton fabric (and, of course, the fish).

Gyotaku, the Japanese art of fish printing, is a similar form. A fish (freshly caught or thawed) can be cleaned with detergent, and then inked. The fish is covered with cloth and then lightly pressed with the fingers. In lieu of real fish, rubber molds are now available through some craft suppliers.

BODY PARTS

The green thumb (from the left hand), caught red-handed, was stamped on cloth.

Inked fingertips are stamped to make flower petals and birds. Details are drawn with permanent pen.

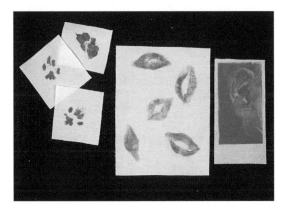

Cat's paws and lips (not the cat's) were inked and printed. The photographic ear was made by pressing warmed PenScore onto an ear, then inking and stamping with the impressed block.

If you have ever been fingerprinted (with a stamp pad), you've used a body part as a stamp. One of the world's oldest stamps, found in primitive rock paintings and caves throughout the world, is the human hand. It is a great stamp for kids, who will love putting a hand in the paint and leaving their personal identification on cloth. A few practice prints will help to determine the optimum amount of paint. Footprints work as well. We tend to think in terms of baby's feet, but prints of a 40-year-old's hands or feet make quite an impact!

Certainly lips have been stamped onto more than one white shirt or innocent cheek for a very personal stamp. Fingertips make good spots or polka dots (remember *How the Leopard Got Its Spots?*) and more than one cat has added paw prints by marching across a worktable. What other body parts you might want to ink up, I leave to your imagination and panache.

Product /Brand Name	Material	Easy to Cut or Tear	Draw or Incise w/Pen or Pencil	Carve w/Knife or Tool	Two Sided	Needs Mounting	Flexible	Self-Adhesive	Thickness	Size	Comments	Sources
Balsa Foam	plastic foam	yes	yes	yes	yes	no	no	no	1/8" up	3"x 3" to 9" x 12"	easy to use, easy to carve	1, 2, 8, 9, 13
Darice Foamies	foam	yes	no	no	yes	yes	yes	no	3mm	9" x 12"	thin sheets	2
Erasers, soft; (Art Gum, Design, Sanford, Faber Castel, Sax, Speedball)	gum eraser	no	no	yes	yes	no	no	no	7/8" to 1" or 1" x 1" x 1"	1" x 1" x 2"		1, 2, 9, 13
Erasers, hard; (Pink Pearl, Mars, Magic Rub, Able-rub, Pencil)	vinyl or plastic	no	no	yes	yes	no	no	no	1/4" up	various	handy, widely available	1, 2, 9, 13
E-Z Cut Blocks	rubber-like	no	no	yes	yes	no	yes	no	1/8" to 3/8"	various	slightly grainy	1, 2, 8, 13
Flexible Printing Plate	vinyl	yes	no	yes	no	no	yes	yes	1/16"	9" x 12"	can print on irregular surface	1, 2, 7, 13
Flexi-Cut printing plates	flexible mat	yes	no	yes	yes	yes	yes	yes	1/16"	various	can print on irregular surface	1, 2, 8, 13
Flexi-Foam	foam	yes	yes	no	yes	yes	yes	no	1/16"	9" x 12"	thin sheets	1, 2
Fun Foam	synthetic foam	yes	yes	yes	yes	yes	yes	no	1/16"	17" x 22"	colored sheets	2, 13
Linoleum Block	linoleum	no	no	yes	no	yes	no	yes	1/16" up	various	usually comes pre-mounted	1, 2, 7, 9, 13
Miracle Sponge cellulose	compressed	yes	no	no	no	no	yes dry	no	1/16"	8" x 11"	good for kids, swells to 3/4"	2, 7, 9
Marscarve	rubber-like	yes	no	yes	yes	no	no	no	1/4"	various		1
PenScore	dense foam	yes	yes	no	yes	both	yes	no	1/8" to 7/8"	8" x 10"	heat to impress design	1, 2, 9, 13
Polyprint Printing Plate	polystyrene foam	yes	yes	no	no	yes	yes	yes	1/8"	9" x 12"	thin sheets	1, 7, 13
Print Foam	polystyrene foam	yes	yes	no	no	no	no	no	1/16" to 1/4"	6" x 9" to 18" x 24"	good for kids, sharp prints	2, 9
Safety-Kut	soft, heavy	no	no	yes	yes	no	yes	no	3/8"	various	easy to carve, fine grained	2, 9
Scratch-Foam Board	printing plate	yes	yes	no	no	no	yes	no	1/16"	9" x 12"	solvent clean ok, thin sheets	2, 9, 13
Soft-Kut	rubber-like	yes	no	yes	yes	no	yes	no	1/4"	various	easy to carve	1, 2, 8, 13
Speedy Cut Print Block	rubber-like	no	no	yes	yes	both	yes	no	1/4"	various	easy to carve	1, 2, 7, 8, 13
Weather-stripping	vinyl foam	yes	no	no	no	yes	yes	yes	various	various	handy, widely available	4

Additional Products

Product	Sources
Brayers, hard plastic	1, 2, 5, 9, 13
soft, foam	2, 8, 9, 13
carvable	2
backgrounds	2, 5, 8, 9, 13
Daubers	1, 2, 5, 8, 13
Sponge Brushes	1, 2, 4, 5, 9

Product	Sources
Discharge Agents	3, 4
Soft Scrub with Bleach	3, 4
Sunlight with Bleach	3, 4
Clorox Clean-up	3, 4
Comet with Chlorinol	3, 4
Storage System, Stamp 'N Stor	15
Thermofax Screens	14

Product	Sources
Alum	3, 4, 9
Sodium Alginate	7, 11
Monagum	11
Resists	7, 11, 12
Synthrapol	7, 11

THE STAMPING PROCESS

CHAPTER 2

Now for the fun—stamping! Put on some lively music and your work shirt. Stamping is a rhythmic activity, and several quilt artists referred to the enjoyment of stamping with music. If you are vexed or irritated, just the physical action of stamping can let off steam as you unwind.

WHAT YOU NEED

PALETTES AND STAMP PADS

A palette is any non-absorbent, smooth, flat surface that will hold the paints and dyes and enable you to mix them for stamping. A plastic plate, a page-sized piece of Plexiglas, a Styrofoam® tray, an aluminum pie tin, a piece of freezer paper (plastic side up), or the lid of a Styrofoam carry-out food container all work well. Some stamps can be touched directly to the palette that serves as a stamp pad. Disposable palettes can be tossed out when you finish, avoiding the need to clean them (this is especially helpful if there is not a convenient water source). You can use a brayer to spread the paint on the palette, as well as to pick up paint to ink the stamp.

Comparing Apples to Oranges,
42" x 53", Wendy Huhn,
Photo: David Loveall Photography

Using old alphabet stamps and a carved apple and orange, Wendy created her tongue-in-cheek panel. The theme grew out of comparisons which, like life, make little sense. She used stamps, stenciling, inkjet, and CLC (color laser copier) transfers, as well as glitter, sequins, and beads.

A traditional stamp pad holds ink or paint for printing by soaking it into fiber or fabric. The pad can be a commercial one (either pre-inked or blank) or it can be a homemade pad. Most commercial stamp pads made for paper are saturated with non-permanent ink. A few, such as Fabrico, are made specifically for cloth. Blank or uninked stamp pads, like Purrfection's, are generally available. Textile paints, which dry faster than inks, are best used on an improvised pad or palette.

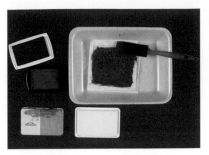

Commercial stamp pads, both inked and uninked, and a home-made stamp pad

To press a stamp directly on the pad, you will need an absorbent surface (such as a muslin or felt pad) to hold the ink. Make one by cutting two or three pieces of fabric or felt about 4" x 5" (larger or smaller, depending upon the size of your stamp). Dip the fabric in water and wring it out or use a brayer to remove excess water. The dampened material absorbs the paint readily and keeps it moist longer. Place the pad on any of the palette surfaces mentioned above, smooth the felt, add paint, and brush to make an even coat. Several layers of muslin, gauze, or cheesecloth will also make a good pad. Or you can omit the ink pad altogether. Use a dauber to ink your stamp directly from the palette.

Detail of *Mary, Mary 4: Buttons* and *Mary, Mary 2: Teapots,* Judith Vierow

When Judith scissor-cut her Printfoam stamp, she put the positive parts of the design on one piece of Plexiglas, and the negative or alternating pieces on another. She then printed one stamp on cloth, followed by the other, inking different colors on different areas. Permaset Fabric Printing Ink was applied with foam and bristle brushes.

PAINTS/DYES

There are dozens of brands of paints, metallics, dyes, acrylics, and inks. Sometimes the terms describing them are used interchangeably. Paint is a generic term for pigment in any of a variety of mediums. Dyes are thin and tend to permeate fabric. Inks are usually thin, but can also be viscous, as with block-printing inks. They may be oil- or water-based, transparent, or nearly opaque. Metallics have a shine or luster. Because of these varying characteristics, information about them has been condensed into a chart. It offers the specific information you need to select paints for your stamping needs.

NAME	FABRICS	CLEAN-UP	HEAT-SET	PERMANENT TO WASHING	CHANGE OF HAND	COMMENTS	REFER TO SOURCE LIST
Createx Multisurface Acrylic	all	water	no	yes	changes slightly	versatile	1, 2, 6, 8, 9, 13
Createx Pigments	all	water	yes	yes	almost no change	extended drying time	1, 2, 6, 8, 9, 13
Daniel Smith Block Printing Ink	all	solvent	no	yes	changes slightly	air dry one month to wash	6
Deka Permanent Fabric Paint	all	water	yes	yes	almost no change	all Deka: versatile,	1, 2, 7, 9, 13
Deka Metallic	all	water	yes	yes	almost no change	easy to use	1, 2, 7, 9, 13
Deka Opaque	all	water	yes	yes	almost no change	array of colors	1, 2, 7, 9, 13
Deka Silk	all	water	yes	yes	soft	neat, easy to use	1, 2, 7, 9, 13
Deka-Print Fabric Printing Paint	all	water	no	no	changes slightly	top quality, intermixable	1, 7, 8
Deka-Print Textile Screening Ink	all	water	yes	yes	changes slightly	use on light-colored fabrics	1, 7, 8, 9
DecoArt Americana Acrylic	all	water	no	yes	slightly stiffening		2
Delta Ceramcoat Acrylic	all	water	no	yes	slightly stiffening	mix with fabric medium	2
Delta Fabric Paint	all	water	yes	yes	changes slightly	flexible, won't crack	2, 9, 12
Delta Stamping Paint	all	water	yes	yes	changes slightly	flexible, won't crack	2, 9, 12
Dr. Ph. Martin's Ready Tex Textile Air Brush Color	all	water	yes	yes	almost no change	vivid colors	8, 9, 13
Folk Art Acrylic	all	water	no	yes	changes slightly	mix with fabric medium	2

Name	Fabrics	Clean-up	Heat-set	Permanent to Washing	Change of Hand	Comments	Refer to Source List
Golden Acrylic	all	water	no	yes	changes slightly	mix with fabric medium	2, 8, 9, 13
InkoDye Concentrated Vat Dye	natural fibers	water	chem-set	yes	none	odor	1, 7, 12
Jacquard Textile Paint	all	water	yes	yes	soft	versatile	1, 7, 12
Lumiere by Jacquard	almost all	water	yes	yes	slightly stiffening	very metallic	1, 7, 12
Metallics by Jacquard	almost all	water	yes	yes	slightly stiffening	very luminescent	1, 7, 12
Neopaque by Jacquard	almost all	water	yes	yes	slightly stiffening	very opaque	1, 7, 12
Liquitex Concentrated Artist Color Acrylic	almost all	water	no	yes	slightly stiffening		1, 2, 7, 9, 10, 13
Liquitex Metallic	almost all	water	no	yes	slightly stiffening		1, 2, 7, 9, 10, 13
NAZ-DAR Textile Screening Ink	all except nylon	solvent	no	yes	slightly stiffening	slow drying	1, 8
Pearl-Ex Mica Pigments	all			yes		add to medium, paints, acrylic, oil	10, 12, 13
PERMASET Textile Paint	all	water	yes	yes	none	odor, slow drying	8
Plaid Fabric Paints	all	water	no	no	changes slightly	fine tips, three dimensional paints	2, 13
PROfab Textile Inks	all naturals & blends	water	yes	yes	none	odorless	1, 11
Procion Fiber Reactive Dyes	natural fibers	water	chem-set	yes	none	powder is toxic	1, 7, 9, 11
Setacolor Fabric Paint	all	water	yes	yes	none	vivid colors	2, 7, 9, 13
Setacolor Transparent	natural fibers	water	yes	yes	none	heliographic	2, 7, 9, 13
Speedball Water Soluble Printing Ink	all	water	no	no	none	odor	1, 8, 13
Tulip Ultra-soft	all	water	no	yes	almost no change	good for use on dark fabrics	2, 7, 8
Versatex Textile Paint	all	water	yes	yes	changes slightly	versatile	1, 7,

Applicators: sponge roller, film canister with weather stripping, daubers, make-up sponges, bristle brushes, and foam brushes

Foam brayer used to ink the stamp

hand: CHUNKY STAMPS

TIP: *Switch to a foam brush, a dauber or a pad for fine lines—avoid a bristle brush.*

TIP: *Sandwich papers will be put to dozens of uses in your workshop. They are inexpensive at restaurant supply stores like Smart & Final.*

APPLICATORS

The applicator is any tool you use for applying the paint directly to your stamp. If you are stamping from a stamp pad or from the palette, you don't need an applicator. To lift paint from the paint jar or palette to ink the stamp, most designers prefer to use a foam brush, daubing the paint lightly on the stamp to achieve an even coat. A dauber offers good control with paint and makes it easy to blend and change colors. An inexpensive dauber or applicator made by Juliana Alspaugh consists of an empty film canister, one end of which has been covered with self-adhesive weatherstripping. Sponges, especially fine-textured ones like cosmetic sponges, make good applicators.

To use a brayer, ink it on the palette and roll it onto the stamp using one continuous motion to avoid any pooling of paint in the crevices of the design.

Some designers prefer to use a flat-bristled brush of medium softness. Stiffer bristles will create more textural lines in the paint surface, but if the stamp design is intricate, a brush may deposit excess paint in the crevices, and this buildup will make the print less clear. Paint can be patted onto the stamp, making shading or blending of colors easy. You may end up with rainbow-hued fingers, so keep a damp cloth handy or wear disposable gloves.

Using Light on Dark

A metallic paint (top left) or an acrylic (bottom right) will cover a dark fabric. Heat-set water-based paints do not cover darks and are best suited to white or light fabrics.

Stamping a light color over dark fabric is complicated by the fact that many paints and dyes are translucent or transparent. Using light over dark is like trying to dye navy fabric yellow. It doesn't work. Here are a few alternatives.

Acrylics, which coat the surface of cloth and are opaque, can be used to print light on dark. Metallics are usually opaque enough to cover a dark background. Versatex and Deka have a "covering white" or opaquer that can be mixed with their paints. Discharge (pages 46-47) gives a light-on-dark effect.

Changing Colors

When changing colors, going from light to dark often saves cleaning the stamp between colors. The switch from yellow, for example, to yellow green, green, and then to blue may require no applicator cleaning between colors. To switch from green to red would require cleaning, or you would end up with brown. The transition from light to dark works, but from dark to light does not. Sometimes stamping a few times on damp paper towels is sufficient cleaning.

To shade or blend colors on a single stamp, daub on paints using the corners of a foam brush. Then use a clean dauber to blend where the colors meet. All-Night Media has inks for fabric that come with a dauber, like shoe polish.

Detail of *Pots and Cups,* Nancy Taylor, full quilt on page 4.

While sponge-brushing paints to her hand-carved stamps, Nancy blended colors to get light-to-dark or magenta-to-purple variations. The variations add depth and brightness to the stamped areas.

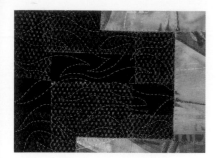

Detail of *Flight,* Maureen Bardusk

FABRIC

Most commercial stamps are made for use on paper. Because paper is smooth, every detail of the stamp will print, whereas fabric, because of its weave, shows a softer image. Cotton, white denim, and muslin are the fabrics most often used, since they are durable, versatile, and available. The smoother the fabric, the more detailed the print. Each fabric has its own character and will influence the look of the print. Stamping on flannel, for example, gives a soft, slightly blurred edge since the paint adheres to some of the nap. A stamp on satin offers a contrast between shiny and dull. Fabrics that are part synthetic may let inks or paints migrate, creating a very different effect. Unusual textures can be created by stamping over heavily textured or transparent fabrics, as seen in a detail of Maureen Bardusk's *Flight.*

TIP: *Use a smooth, ironed fabric if you want to have a sharp image (no starch or spray finish). Folds or wrinkles will affect clarity.*

Flight, 30" x 46", Maureen Bardusk

The fabric texture creates its own pattern when a blank linoleum block is inked and stamped over it. By printing overlapping blocks in both gold and silver metallic paints, a transparent effect is created. Within the gently arcing dark and light pattern, Maureen stamped a block marked with wipe-out tools (page 34). Curved lines are appliquéd, and a bottle cork provided the stamp for the small white circles. Final stamps were added after quilting. The furrows of quilt stitches resist the ink. Maureen uses Jacquard Textile Paint and Liquitex Metallic and non-metallic acrylic.

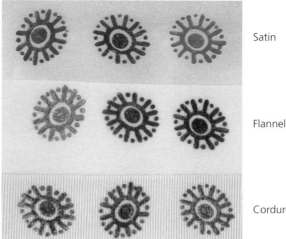

Satin

Flannel

Corduroy

All washable fabrics should be washed before stamping to pre-shrink them and remove substances (dust, lint, oil from handling, sizing, etc.) that may interfere with the paint's adherence. Even if the finished piece will never be washed, a fabric that is not pre-shrunk may draw up or warp slightly from a water-based paint. Some designers, however, prefer to use unwashed cottons, since the sizing adds crispness that makes them easier to handle. If the fabric has water-repellant, non-wrinkling, or similar finishes (and is not pre-washed), some paints may bleed on the surface.

Always check your inks or paints to make sure they are compatible with your fabric. Natural fibers (silk, cotton, cellulose rayon, linen) may require a different paint than what you use on acetate rayon or polyester. If the paint needs to be heat-set, then the fabric must be able to withstand the heat required.

Transparent Fabrics

Transparent fabrics need to be handled carefully, since some ink will seep directly through the open weave to whatever is beneath it. If the fabric shifts at all, ink may transfer or smear to the back of the panel. To avoid smears, tape the sheer fabric down so that it can't slide. After stamping, lift the sheer so that it doesn't stick to the work surface as it dries. Once it's dry, re-tape for a second stamping or for overlapping shapes. Or lay the sheer down on a fabric-covered table (muslin or flannel). Pin or tape if necessary. The fabric surface absorbs any paint that seeps through. Paper towels will also absorb extra paint.

I've ironed freezer paper to the back of some sheers (Be sure your sheer can withstand the heat). Paper keeps the fabric from moving, prevents smearing, and resists the ink. If the fabric is pulled off the paper immediately, care must be taken to avoid letting the wet paint area touch anything. An extra pair of hands is helpful.

White-on-White Prints

White-on-white fabrics are printed with an opaque paint that resists any transparent color used over them. This can be used to create patterns within stamped images. When Pele Fleming stamped transparent color onto white-on-white fabric, the printed white resisted the color, giving the impression that tiny prints were used throughout.

When white-on-white fabric prints are stamped, some of the white pattern shows through the stamped color since the white print tends to resist the paint.

TIP: *Before starting any large project, test the paint and fabric you intend to use.*

Window Hanging, 15" x 8",
Lorna Lawson

The see-through silk organza used on this panel is stamped with Jacquard Metallics.

Detail of *Garden of Eden II,* Pat White

Pat cut these bird stamps from felt and glued them to a block of wood with a waterproof adhesive. She stamped the birds on polyester tulle, using Setacolor Transparent developed in sunlight. The tulle was appliquéd over stamped and printed areas and stitched to create a smooth transition between fabrics. Triangles and bars were cut from self-adhesive foam board and mounted on wood blocks.

TIP: *Keep several damp paper towels on hand while you are working. Any stamp not in use can be placed face down on the damp paper towels and will stay moist.*

CARE AND USE OF STAMPS

CARE AND CLEANING

Stamps have long lives ahead of them if given proper care. Many of us are still using lettering sets from our childhood. Signature stamps from the Victorian era can still be found and museums house collections of cylindrical seals and ancient stamps, so they do last!

Cleaning stamps carefully is important. If paint dries in the recesses of an image it will be almost impossible to remove.

When you are ready to clean up, hold the stamp under running water and use a soft-bristled toothbrush on the hard-to-reach crevices. Be aware, however, that excessive scrubbing can damage details of your stamp. Using a soft sponge for cleaning may take a bit longer, but will be safer. Blot and dry. Don't immerse wood stamps in water.

STORAGE

Store rubber stamps with the rubber side down, out of direct sunlight, and away from excessive heat, since rubber can harden and decompose. Sponge stamps need to be dry before placing them in storage and must be face-up, or on a smooth surface so that the sponge is not compressed.

If you get enthusiastic about stamping, you will eventually need to consider storage. Sliding trays or drawers are wonderful for offering a look at an entire drawer at once. Clear plastic boxes work well. Dozens of commercial storage units are now on the market. Stamp 'N Stor Mounting System offers a way to store your handmade stamps. The cushion is attached to a cling vinyl, which can be peeled off after use and applied to a storage board. Or, you can simply dump all your stamps into a box. That way, you can always "discover" new stamps in the bottom of the box! Some stamps, like CHUNKY STAMPS have handles and can be hung. I keep mine (those on acrylic blocks) in flat white boxes, and then stamp the images on top so I can see at a glance what's inside.

PRINTING SURFACE AND WORK SPACE

Your back will give out long before your paint supply, unless you find a comfortable way to work. A firm, stable surface at a convenient working height is essential. If you work sitting down, then table height is fine. If you prefer to work standing, as I do, then use a counter or raise your worktable. Even two 4x4s under the ends of the table legs will make a big difference.

Cover your work area before starting any project. Freezer paper (paper side up) is my preference since nothing can seep through. It can be tossed out when you have finished and it provides a paper surface on which to test your stamps! Most fiber artists prefer a hard surface to stamp on. My preference is for light padding, so I bought an inexpensive kitchen table from a discount store, added a layer of flannel, then a layer of muslin, turned it upside down, and stapled everything securely to the underside. The muslin helps hold fabric in place for stamping. I find the slight give is helpful, especially if I am printing from old alphabets which have hardened somewhat. With foam stamps, a harder surface is preferable. A piece of shirt cardboard offers a good, smooth surface when a small workspace is needed. For a larger area, use a sheet of foamcore board — it's lightweight, smooth, and firm, and can be covered with freezer paper.

Having a sink handy for the work area is ideal, but in lieu of one, a small bucket of water will do fine. If you have to clean up your work area so your house can function (if you work on the kitchen table), get some transparent plastic storage bins so that you can move it all in one or two trips.

Good lighting is essential. If you are using paints that require heat-setting, keep your iron nearby. A thrift-shop iron (old, heavy, and no steam vents) is great. A 9" x 12" plywood board covered with flannel, then muslin, makes a perfect pressing board to keep right on your worktable.

QUILTING

Stamped fabric can be quilted with an all-over pattern like any other print. Stamping done after quilting will give an effect quite different from stamping done before quilting. Quilting will leave a furrow or channel along the stitches too deep for a stamp to reach and will create breaks or interruptions in the stamped image. This will always be a part of the look of pieces stamped after quilting.

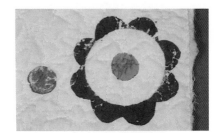

After quilting, the uneven surface of the material interferes with stamping, creating textures and open areas.

Stamped before quilting, the image is clearer. Quilting outlines the stamp in this sample.

Detail of *At Home on the Ranges,*
June Brown

A detail of June's panel shows her map of Australia stamped over a section of background. The cut-out kangaroo stamps overlap all the construction lines as well as lines of quilting.

Detail of *Zebra Dance,* Karen Page

For this quilt's border, Karen combined hand quilting with stamping to create a continuous pattern. Striped areas within the quilt are made with torn paper over which she has used a screening process. She stamped with a Fabrico® ink pad.

zebra: CHUNKY STAMPS

Detail of *Hopscotch Heaven,* Elaine Plogman, full quilt on page 62.

Elaine uses quilting to enhance the geometric shapes of her stamped designs by stitching on the edge of the stamp. A second line of quilting echoes the edge of the stamp.

Quilting can enhance the stamped images themselves, as in Elaine Plogman's *Hopscotch Heaven*. Here each edge of the image has a parallel quilting line that enhances the design and generates a relief surface. In Nancy Taylor's *Pots and Cups* (page 4), the quilting lines are close to the edge of the print. In *Sticks and Stones* (page 13), the quilting falls just at the edge of the stamp. In Pele Fleming's *Rain Forest Frog Quilt* she hand quilted the pieced areas, avoiding any quilting over the stamps (page 40).

Stamps can be used to mark quilting lines. Susan Smeltzer dipped a weatherstripping stamp in water, then lightly pressed it onto a paper towel and then more firmly onto fabric. The edge of the wet line was machine quilted and by the time that area was finished the fabric was dry. The stamp was then re-wetted to mark the next area. Enough water is needed to moisten the fabric, which changes its color slightly, but not enough to soak it or let the water run. The *Spiral Pillows* (page 70) were quilted this way.

Sharon Doyle used another method to mark her quilt. First she stamped a butterfly on tear-away paper, then she positioned that paper butterfly on her panel. After machine quilting the butterfly, she tore the paper away, leaving the relief design on the cloth.

Stamp a figure on cloth. Stamp additional figures on paper and cut out (on right).

Stamp butterfly on tear-away paper.

butterfly: Graphistamp

Position on layered fabrics, then quilt.

Cover and protect the printed figure on fabric with a paper cutout.

Remove tear-away paper

Quilted butterfly design

Stamp a second figure on fabric, remove the paper, and the second girl appears to be behind the first.

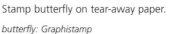

Sharon stamped her butterfly twice to get a strong, as well as lighter impression. A third butterfly was stamped on paper, placed on the panel, and quilted using the tear-away method. This teaching sample also includes hand painting and quilting that echoes the curves of the butterfly antennae.

butterfly: Stampa Barbara

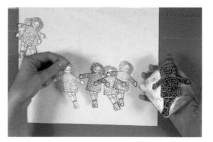

Now cover both figures with paper and stamp a third one.

Continue the process to create an entire crowd.

MASKING

Masking provides a means of using only a portion of a stamp, or of combining stamps. It protects an area from the inked stamp as a second imprint is made. If you stamp one horse on fabric and another on paper, you can then cut out the paper horse and place it over the one on fabric. When you stamp a second horse on fabric, overlapping the first, part of the ink will be on the cloth and part on the paper. Remove the paper and you now have a team of horses, one behind the other, and you will be on your way to having a whole herd.

Another good masking material is freezer paper, which can be heat-tacked in place. It is particularly convenient if your arrangement gets complex and several masks are needed at once.

Freezer paper or contact paper masks can be applied to cloth leaving open or negative areas. Once this open area is heavily and randomly stamped, the mask is removed, and the open space is now a positive shape. The cat in the example that follows emerges in a textural pattern.

Stamp a window frame image onto fabric.

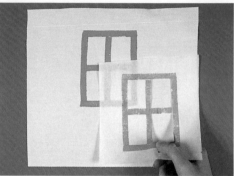

Stamp a second window on tracing paper and cut out and remove one window pane.

Stamp a figure inside the window.

woman: Fruit Basket Upset

Cut out another pane and repeat the process with the cat—the paper cut-out is at left.

cat: Robert Bloombury

Stamp multiple images in the windows, covering and protecting the areas not being stamped.

pig: Nature Impressions; chicken: unknown origin; black cat: Robert Bloombury; woman: Fruit Basket Upset

Canned Goods, 6½" x 12½",
Sharon Doyle

After stamping a jar on cotton fabric, Sharon stamped a second jar on a masking material (freezer paper). She cut out the paper jar shape, keeping the outside or negative shape, which she ironed onto her fabric to expose only the inside of the jar. When she stamped the insects next, any that went past the edge of the jar were stamped on the protective paper. That jar was masked as she stamped the next jar and the process was repeated. Zigi and NIJI® fabric ink markers were used for added color.

jar: A.N.T. Transfer; clouds, dragonfly: unknown; wings, bats, butterfly: Stampa Barbara; airplane: The Stamp Pad Co, Inc; balloons: Co-Motion; angel: Rubber Stamps of America; fairy: Hero Arts; fly: Bizzaro; flying saucer: Stamp Crazy

A tree form cut from freezer paper was ironed onto cloth. It was stamped over all edges, so that when the freezer paper was peeled away the contour of the tree appeared. Stamps created the negative area.

tree: PSX (Personal Stamp Exchange)

The cat was cut from freezer paper and the background shape was ironed onto fabric. The cat was stamped with acrylics, using two custom-made stamps. When the freezer paper was peeled away the cat emerged.

Poppies, 11" x 11½", Sharon Doyle

Complex masking is used to accommodate various overlays. The two lower flowers were stamped on fabric. Additional flowers on paper were cut out to mask the two stamped flowers so the basket could be stamped. All stamped images were masked while more poppies were added until the arrangement was complete. Finally, markers were used for highlights.

TIP: *To mask small areas, use Post-it® notes, being sure not to cut away the entire sticky strip on the back. These can be pulled off and re-used.*

WIPE-OUT TOOLS

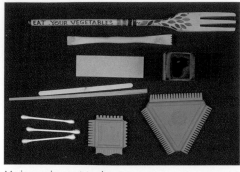

Various wipe-out tools

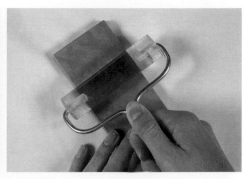

Printing block inked with brayer to provide all-over area of color.

Wipe-out tool used over inked block to remove paint and create design.

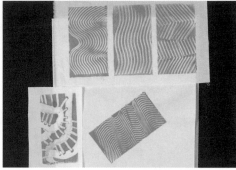

Prints of the designs

When using any uncarved stamp or block, an option is to do a negative, printing the background rather than the image. If you brush or brayer paint on a block, and then draw an X on it with your finger, you can remove, or wipe-out some paint. Like a "dust me" sign left on a smooth dark table by some too-observant friend. If you then print the block on fabric, you would print an area with a light X. This principle has dozens of variations.

Maureen Bardusk uses wipe-out tools to great effect in the background of *Stratum* (page 63), with linoleum blocks providing background textured area. Good wipe-out tools include palette knives, sticks, mastic scrapers, ceramic tools, or anything in sight that will wipe or pull paint off the surface. Another way of removing ink is to press an un-inked stamp against an inked block. This removes the image of the stamp and makes a reverse print of it.

REGISTRATION AND ALIGNMENT

Fabric, unlike paper, stretches, gives, and moves readily, so the inevitable variation from one stamped image to another might as well be welcomed. Each print is slightly different in terms of paint coverage, and each will vary slightly in placement. Recognizing all that, there are times when more accurate placement is significant to the design.

Random

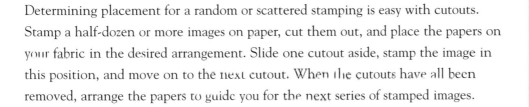

For a random, all-over pattern, stamp first on paper. Cut out those images and place them on fabric in the desired arrangement.

hand: CHUNKY STAMPS

Determining placement for a random or scattered stamping is easy with cutouts. Stamp a half-dozen or more images on paper, cut them out, and place the papers on your fabric in the desired arrangement. Slide one cutout aside, stamp the image in this position, and move on to the next cutout. When the cutouts have all been removed, arrange the papers to guide you for the next series of stamped images.

Align inked stamp over paper, then slip paper out and stamp cloth.

TIP: *When printing onto squares of fabric for quilt blocks, always cut the fabric a little larger than needed. That way, you can trim the stamped block to keep the image centered.*

TIP: *Keep in mind that if you are stamping suns or stars, direction won't matter—if it is houses or trees, it might.*

Lines

For a border or straight line of stamps, a guide is helpful. One possibility is to press a fold in your fabric where you want the lower edge of the stamp to be aligned. Lightly press the fold so the crease is still visible but does not have a raised ridge. Then align the bottom edge of the stamp with the crease to achieve a straight line of stamped images.

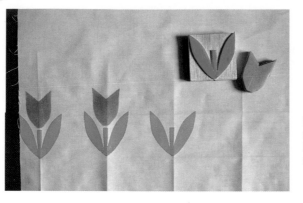

Light, vertical creases mark the spacing between stamps. Horizontal creases guide placement of the tops of the leaves.

To space border stamps an equal distance apart, you will again need a guide. Measure the width of the stamp, add the space you want between images, and mark those increments on your fabric or a card guide. A light pencil line or a slight crease will do.

Pencil lines on a card guide in the placement of stamps.

sun: Imprints Graphic Studio

Another aid to alignment and spacing is to use cards cut to the width of the stamp plus whatever space is desired between them. Place two cards, side by side, at one side of the stamped image. Remove the first card and the opening indicates the placement for the stamp. The free card then leapfrogs over the second, which is in turn removed.

After stamping, the second hen, move the lefhand card to the far right and repeat the process as cards leapfrog across your fabric.

hen: unknown origin

All-Over Prints

To stamp images in an all-over pattern requires careful attention. If the stamps are square, or have a straight edge, a T-square may be all the guide you need.

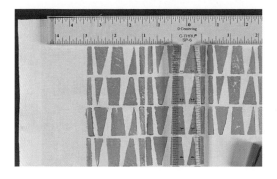

T-square and edge of the stamps guide in placement for all-over pattern.

To align shaped blocks, the greatest single help is to have the base of the block cut to the shape and size of the image. That way you can see exactly where one stamp fits next to the other. Katy Jane Widger's tessellated arched stamps are made this way (page 45). Clear bases simplify alignment.

When edge of design is also edge of stamp, placement is simplified.

For an all-over pattern, a grid will help with alignment. Guides will be needed for both horizontal and vertical placement.

Light pencil line guides placement.

If you need to stamp in the very center of a fabric block, first stamp an image on paper, cut it out, and place it on the fabric. Mark the center point of the fabric on each side, as well as at the top and bottom. Some designers do this with a light crease at the edges—others use a pencil mark. Next you will need to indicate corresponding lines on the stamp. The schoolhouse at right shows lines on a sheet of Mylar to which a stamp is attached. These lines are simply matched to fabric creases or pencil lines. Another marking method is to draw lines on the sides and base of the stamp, aligning them to folds or marks on the fabric.

Identify the center on each edge of the stamp and mark it. Here a marking pen was used on Plexiglas. Then identify the center of your fabric and mark it. The two can then be aligned.

Each image will be stamped in exactly the same position on each identically cut piece of fabric.

Flexi-Cut schoolhouse stamp mounted on double-sided adhesive cushion and adhered to Mylar, has black lines drawn for centering and registration.

Two carved stamps used in fabric sample below.

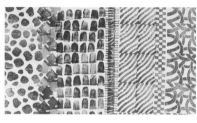

Fabric Sample, Rosemary Hoffenberg

With Deka Fabric Paint and a foam brush, Rosemary can control the density of each print. The entwined loops are from a linoleum block, the checkerboard is a Soft-Kut printing block, the diagonal stripes are carved Balsa Foam glued to a block of wood. There are also brush strokes, more stamps, and linoleum block prints.

Fabric Sample, Rosemary Hoffenberg

A spiral design carved in a linoleum block was inked, then stamped twice to create a secondary or shadow image. Triangles are double-stamped wood scraps, salvaged from a workshop floor. Between these two triangles is a pattern of brush strokes.

The Balsa Foam diagonals and linoleum block spiral were used in the fabrics above.

In Praise of Old Women, 32" x 30", Sharon Doyle

After stamping the woman's face and the roses onto hand-dyed cloth, Sharon highlighted areas with a permanent marker. Her stamped fabrics are combined with piecing and *broderie perse* to create the composition. The border quote is from Harriet Beecher Stowe. The quilt, in honor of Sharon's grandmother, Rose, was printed with brown fabric ink.

face: Granny Moon; roses: PSX (Personal Stamp Exchange); alphabet: vintage

STAMPED LETTERS

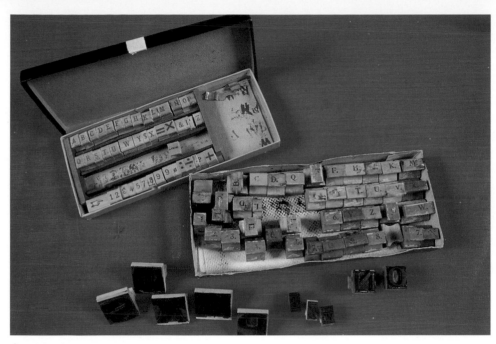

CHAPTER 3

A variety of alphabet stamps

Our first forays into stamping were probably with alphabet sets. It was magical, making whole words appear, or jumbling letters in nonsensical patterns. Even building blocks had bright enameled letters that left impressions in clay (or mud!).

Many fiber artists use words and letters to enhance, clarify, or expand the content of their pieces, while others use lettering as a central focus. Karen Berkenfeld (page 44) stamps words on fabric and then collages them onto her panel. In *Sojourner Truth* (page 42) lettering is the heart of the quilt. Images and words merge and reinforce one another in Pele Fleming's work, (page 40).

One of the most memorable gifts I ever received was a stamped set of dishtowels, but instead of the prosaic seven days of the week, these were emblazoned with the seven deadly sins. "Gluttony," "Greed," and "Sloth" were artfully embroidered around the large and simple alphabet letters. They add a certain panache to drying the dishes.

However they are used, letters and words give another level of meaning, adding humor, information, or personal viewpoints.

The Soul of Coffee, 23" x 16½", Jody House

Using an alphabet set for stamping, Jody named her favorite blends, adding a coffee brewer's methods at left and at right, with options at the bottom. Small decorative squares were hand carved and stamped. While these cups were Thermofaxed (page 51), they could also be cut from Flexi-Foam or PenScore.

alphabet, small stamps: Columbia-Sign and Chart Printers

The Robot Flies Away, 40" x 30", Kathy Weaver

Using permanent ink, Kathy stamped the quilt's title onto one of a series about the robot's adventures.

Rainforest Frog Quilt, 12½" x 12", Pele D. Fleming

The stamped ecological message in Pele's pond runs rings around the pieced pattern, all in tree-frog green. The frogs, stamped in black on white, were layered, stitched, cut out, and hand colored with permanent markers. They were then attached with tack stitches to the surface of the panel.

frog: Purrfection

Plain Brown Wrappers, 37½" x 30½", Marjorie A. DeQuincy

The plain brown wrapper becomes a plane wrapper in Marjorie's piece full of puns. Stenciled letters are inked and a horse is textured by pulling the stamp up from ink on a palette.

airplane, monkey, small letters, bear: Rubber Stampede; train and horse: CHUNKY STAMPS; paper bag: Azadi Stamp Designs

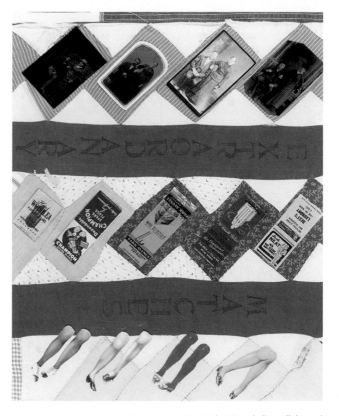

Detail of *Git,* Betsy Nimock, Photo: Betsy Nimock

When she came across two escaped-convict posters in an antique mall, Betsy found the eyes of the fugitive pleading for an advocate. She combined the poster with fragments of a pre-Civil War quilt, and then stamped "Fugitive" across the front. After she stamped the word, she noticed that "git" appeared on the photo, giving the title to the piece. Betsy used an old stamp pad and letters from the 1920s.

Extraordinary Matches, 20" x 16", Jim Nick Nimock (in collaboration with his grandmother, Betsy Nimock), Photo: Betsy Nimock

Eleven-year-old Jimmy chose his title to reflect a visual play on words. Vintage matches, Victorian paper doll legs, and nineteenth-century wedding photos are all seen as extraordinary matches. The collection was applied to fragments of an old quilt, and he stamped the letters from a vintage alphabet and stamp pad.

Penny Saver, 20" x 16", Justin Nimock (in collaboration with his grandmother, Betsy Nimock), Photo: Betsy Nimock

1930s coin collector cards, vintage rubber stamps, and tiny 48-star flags recall collections of days gone by. Sixteen-year-old Justin, who has saved his own pennies since he was a boy, was drawn to this memorabilia. The stamped message (in itself vintage) was done with an old stamp set.

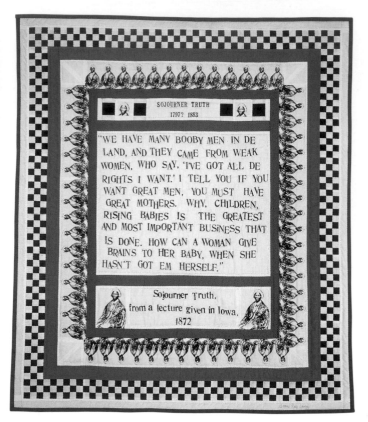

Sojourner Truth, 46" x 40", Jean Ray Laury

A quotation from Sojourner Truth was stamped first on paper to work out the arrangement, then stamped on fabric using permanent black ink and an ink pad. It is surrounded by screen-printed images.

alphabet: Superior's Print Craft

Detail of *Talkin' Baseball,* Heather Urquhart

Intermingled with her Chinese Coins pattern, Heather included over 90 expressions and nicknames used in baseball. The stamped slogans and words merge into the overall pattern, becoming readable at close view. She used a felt stamp pad coated with Versatex.

alphabet: Standard Rubber Type Co. Ltd.

Santa Barbara Claus, 24" x 40", Jan Inouye

Inspired by warm-weather southern California Christmases, Jan gave two of her Santas the sunglasses they'd need. Letters are a crucial part of the composition as well as the content. It's the season for shorts, sunglasses, sandals—and bells. Jan used permanent ink with a disposable, paper-towel stamp pad.

Detail of *Today's Identity,* Susan R. Macy

Pockets of this jacket are stamp printed with names of family and friends (page 53).

ALL-OVER PATTERNS

CHAPTER 4

Repeated as all-over or continuous patterns, stamps can be used to create yardage. The designs can be randomly patterned over the fabric or they can be structured in grids or rows.

Katy Jane Widger, who designs stamps, creates many that are interlocking and can be used in close repeat to create wonderful effects. See below and page 45.

Jeanne Williamson designs and cuts many of her own stamps in 1" art gum blocks and creates grid patterns. She overlaps simple stamps in varying colors, creating new images and patterns within the grid. June Brown's kangaroos leap all over the back of her quilt (page 30), creating a printed fabric that grows out of the stamped blocks she designed for the quilt top.

Therese May's fabric is exuberantly patterned and free from constraints, combining stamps with hand-painted elements (page 45).

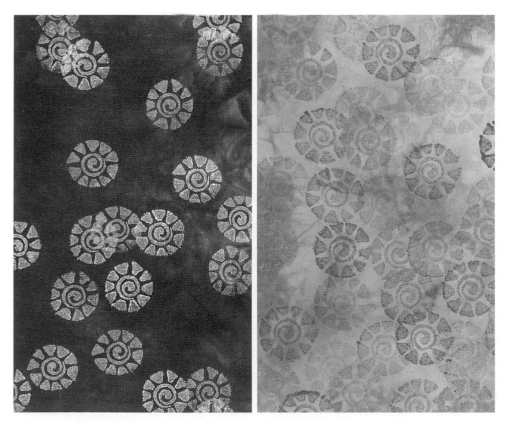

Stamped Fabric, Katy Jane Widger
Katy's own stamp designs are used in overlapping patterns to create depth.

Generation, 36" x 57",
Karen Felicity Berkenfeld

Karen stamps fabric in all-over patterns, then cuts it up for collage. Some of this fabric was stamped using an alphabet of large wooden-handled letters found in an antique shop. For the smaller alphabet she made stamp pads from flat foam sheets, using PERMASET, a slow-drying block-printing ink. The quote, from John F. Kennedy's inauguration speech, is stamped in the small letters on organza and hand stitched to leave frayed edges.

large alphabet, antique stamps: unknown origin; small alphabet: All Night Media

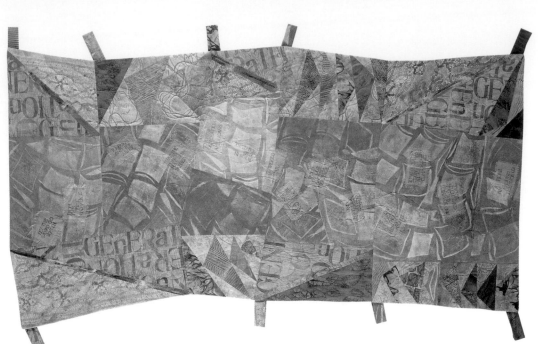

Fabric Sample, Rosemary Hoffenberg

Intertwining loops carved into a linoleum block are repeated here for an all-over pattern. Rosemary offset the block by rotating it to avoid an exact repeat.

Detail of *Do Not Walk All Over Your Mother*, Kathleen Deneris

With a hot knife, Kathleen cut flower shapes from packaging Styrofoam, and glued them to a block. To create a positive/negative effect she contrasted flowers stamped with paints to those that are resist printed. After stamping with starch resist (page 50) she painted the area with NAZ-DAR, later removing the paste to reveal light-colored flowers.

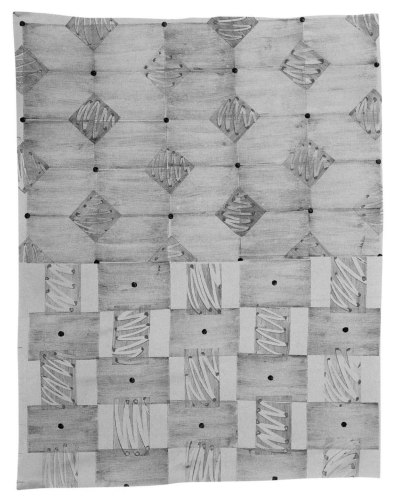

Fabric Sample, Maureen Bardusk

Blank, uncarved 6" x 4" linoleum blocks, painted with a somewhat dry brush, were used for these fabric samples. The wipe-out tool (page 34) was a double-ended stick with rubber ends (one end is pointed, the other is wedge-shaped).

Fabric Samples, Katy Jane Widger

These tessellated designs, part of a series by Katy, interlock in various ways to create wonderful all-over patterns. She stamps with Pro-Textile Inks.

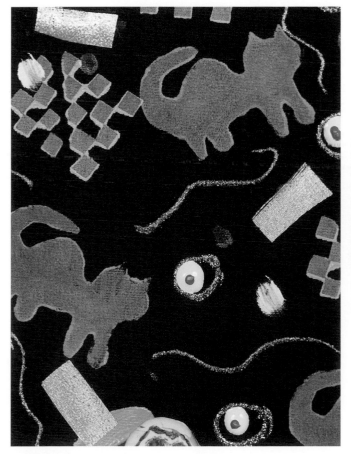

Eraser Prints, Jeanne Williamson

Using an X-Acto knife on 1"-square art gum erasers, Jeanne cut geometric designs, which she stamped in transparent overlays to create new shapes and colors.

Fabric Sample, Therese May

Therese printed this colorful, playful fabric using her own rubber stamps made from sheet rubber. Liquitex acrylic paints, mixed with the gel medium, were applied with a brush. Therese also brush paints directly onto her fabric and adds acrylic motifs so thick that they are three-dimensional on her cloth.

OTHER THINGS YOU CAN DO WITH STAMPS

CHAPTER 5

Detail of Wishes, Promises and Vows,
Ingrid Law

Squares of sticky-back weatherstripping
stuck to Plexiglas makes up the 4"-
square design used on red cotton fabric.
It was appliquéd to the purple rectangle.
The horse, a child's toy, and leaf were
created using bleach discharge (pages
46-47).

Small Bag, 16" x 6", ReNeé Page

ReNeé discharged her designs on navy
rayon with Sunlight automatic dishwasher
detergent used directly from the bottle.
When contrast was achieved, she used a
stop-agent. The stamp for the crisscross
warp and weft lines was a toy tractor part
that ReNeé says is "Great...I can roll it."

flower: CHUNKY STAMPS

Stamp designs can be enlarged, reduced, or collaged. They can be reworked and transferred to silkscreen or laser transfer. Play with them—no need to limit yourself! You can stamp with liquids other than paints; discharge, resist, food dyes, or adhesives. Food-coloring hearts could be sponge-stamped on brie or on a sandwich for Valentine's day—rolled cookie dough could be stamped with holly leaves before Christmas baking. The holly leaves survive baking especially well if food dye is mixed with egg yolk before stamping.

DISCHARGE

By substituting a discharge gel for paint, you can remove color in specific patterns instead of adding it. The gel must contain chlorine bleach and the fabric color must be dischargeable. If you dye your own fabrics with Procion or other fiber-reactive dye, it will readily discharge. When you work with commercial fabrics, use a drop of bleach to test the cloth for its colorfastness. Discharge is more successful with simple, large stamps. Fine, detailed designs will lose some definition as the bleach spreads.

> **Warning:** *Use bleach only outdoors or with adequate ventilation. Protective gloves and facemasks are recommended. Do not return utensils or measuring spoons to the kitchen.*

A simple and safe discharge method utilizes liquid cleanser or gel that contains bleach. Comet® Liquid Gel, Clorox® Clean-up® Gel, Soft Scrub® Liquid Gel, and Sunlight® Automatic Dishwasher Detergent (thickened) are among brands that many artists use. Place a few tablespoons of gel on your palette. Dip a foam brush into the liquid and tamp it onto the stamp. Then press the stamp onto dischargeable cotton or rayon fabric.

Liquid gels contain little bleach, and will therefore work slowly. Watch for changes in color. When the fabric bleaches to the desired degree, use a stop-agent (see the following recipes) to keep it from bleaching further.

STOP-AGENT RECIPES

Both of the following recipes will arrest the bleaching process after discharge.

Solution 1.	Solution 2.
Mix: 1 part vinegar to	Mix: 1/2 cup 3% hydrogen peroxide
1 part water	1 quart of water
This recipe varies a lot and ranges from 1:1 to 1:4 (1 part vinegar to 4 parts water).	A more dilute vinegar rinse (1:20) is sometimes used after the hydrogen peroxide soak.

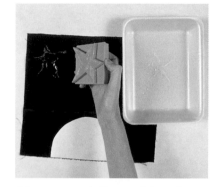

A freezer paper half-moon is ironed onto fabric as a resist. A star stamp, dipped in gel-bleach, is stamped on the fabric. It will require time to discharge.

Either solution will neutralize the bleaching, but a weaker solution may require more time. The discharged fabric must be immersed in a stop-agent, followed by a thorough washing. Running it through the wash cycle helps, as agitation assists in removing the bleach.

THICKENERS

In lieu of a liquid gel, bleach can be added directly to a thickener.

Mix:

Bleach with

Monagum (available at Pro Chemical, page 92)
OR
Sodium alginate (available at Dharma Trading Company, page 92)

As stars discharge and become more visible, the freezer paper is removed to disclose the solid black area that was protected.

star: CHUNKY STAMPS

Follow directions for mixing the thickener and experiment with bleach amounts to get the desired strength.

Cut a design from freezer paper and iron it onto your fabric (or cut one from contact paper and fingerpress it on). Then, using a sponge, stamp the thickened bleach over the exposed fabric. Avoid saturating the fabric, as it will bleed under the edge of the paper. Several light bleachings are easier to handle than one that is too heavy.

ReNeé Page's small bag (page 46) was discharged with stamps, as was *Sticks and Stones* (page 13).

Wishes, Promises and Vows, 28" x 69", Ingrid Law

Resist (pages 48-50), stamping, hand painting, dyeing, embroidery and metallic foiling (page 48) all found their way into this panel. Ingrid also stamped foiling adhesive (page 48) directly to the cloth, let it dry, and then pressed on the foil.

TIP: *Add Synthropol™ to the final washing to keep dye particles in suspension and prevent the redeposit of any dye.*

The heart stamp was coated with Foil-on Textile Transfer Adhesive and stamped onto fabric.

METALLIC FOILS

Iron-on metallics, made for use on paper and cloth, adapt readily for stamping. They all work with an adhesive that is applied to cloth. Once the adhesive is dry, a metallic foil is pressed on and the transfer is made. The smoother the fabric, the glossier the metallic surface.

Among the adhesives that work well are Jones Tones, Aleene's® Foiling Glue, and Foil-on Textile Transfer Adhesive. Metallics are available in a wide range of colors and patterns, including optical effects and rainbow colors. Foil-on Textile Transfer Adhesive suggests the use of a heat press, but I've also had good results in placing fabric over a hard surface and burnishing with the bowl of a spoon. For small areas, the flat part of the fingernail is a good burnisher.

Martie Carroll's silk scarf on page 57 uses metallic foils in its design.

RESIST

Back detail of *Yellow Leaves,* Kathleen Deneris

Trees are created with paste resist stamped onto the fabric. After the background is painted and dried, the paste is removed to reveal the stamped trees in the original fabric color.

Yellow Leaves, 45" x 28", Kathleen Deneris

A grocery store Styrofoam container provided the stamp material for the trees. Kathleen stamped leaves using NAZ-DAR textile paints. Over the background textures of hand painting and starch resist, she quilted spirals, curls, and swirling lines.

Getting the Boot, 22" x 32",
Kathleen Deneris

Both the fish and boot were cut from Printfoam, with details added by drawing directly on the surface. Intricate linear patterns were achieved with potato dextrin crackle resist (page 49) over which Kathleen dragged a large-toothed comb.

Paste resist (or crackle resist) works on the principle that the paint or color applied over a resist will not be absorbed. Once the resist paste has dried and crackled, color is added over the crackled areas. Color seeps through the cracks to create a pattern of fine lines. Once the resist is removed, the background (original) color is again evident. The paste is thick enough to stamp with, though it is more often used over stamped or printed patterns to add background texture.

Kathleen Deneris, who works extensively with resists, uses the following recipe. It is a good idea to designate specific cooking utensils for your craft projects and keep them separate from the ones you use for food. It is usually a good idea to avoid using aluminum, since it can react to some ingredients.

CRACKLE RESIST

1^1/$_3$ cups potato dextrin; available at Rupert, Gibbon, and Spider; Pro Chemical, Dharma Trading Company (see page 92) or a health food store

1 cup boiling water

Sprinkle dextrin in hot water until completely dissolved. Apply warm paste to fabric that has been stretched onto a frame or spread out on a firm surface. As it dries, crackles will appear. Heat-set in an oven at 275° for 6 minutes or until completely dry. Apply textile paint with a foam roller or brush so the ink seeps into the crackle pattern. Heat-set the textile paint in an oven at the temperature recommended by the manufacturer. To remove the resist, soak the fabric in cool water. Place on newsprint and use a spatula to scrape off the resist. Discard resist.

Warning: *Do not allow the scraped off paste to go down the sink drain.*

Kathleen offers another resist recipe that came from the book *African Textile Arts*.

TIP: *The thickness of the resist layer determines the scale of the crackle pattern.*

TIP: *If you are working on a fabric with lots of texture, eliminate the starch as it will make the resist more difficult to wash out.*

SIMPLE RESIST

3 Tbs. flour (any kind)

$1/2$ tsp. alum (available at the drug store)

1 Tbs. powdered laundry starch

1 cup cold water

Blend flour, alum, and starch; add a little water to make a paste. Continue to add water, stir until blended. Place liquid in the top of a double boiler. Cook and stir until the mixture is transparent. Apply to fabric.

The inclusion of starch helps retain the sharp edges of any prints it is used over. Wash in water to remove resist.

CRAYON RESIST

Crayon rubbings over a stamp

Detail of *Wallhanging,* Sherrill Kahn, full quilt shown on page 63

Crayons can be used to provide a resist to water-based paints. Place a stamp under the fabric on which you are working. Hold the stamp firmly, or secure the fabric so that it cannot move. Rub a crayon back and forth over the stamp to deposit wax in the stamp image. Paint in a contrasting color can then be added. The paint will soak into the unwaxed areas. The waxed areas will resist the paint. When dry, remove the crayon by placing the fabric between two layers of paper toweling, and ironing.

Acrylic paints will also work as a resist. When stamped onto fabric and dried, the acrylic-covered area is resistant to any other water-based paint or ink. No crackle effect results. Sherrill Kahn utilizes the resistant qualities of acrylics beautifully in her complex pieces.

Another simple resist is the opaque ink used in printing white-on-white fabrics. When the white-on-white print is stamped with translucent colors, the painted pattern resists the stamped color, giving a two-color print effect (page 27).

THERMOFAX

For those who do Thermofax printing, images can be stamped, grouped, and altered on paper, enlarged on a copier, and imaged in a Thermofax machine. The machine makes what amounts to a photo silkscreen of your image, which can be printed in any color. The image must have strong black and white contrast to create a clear image. Thermofax screens can be made up from your images, or purchased ready-to-go, like stamps, from Spittin' Image. See Source List (# 9), page 92.

A two-inch figure on an acrylic block was stamped, enlarged twice, and then imaged on a Thermofax screen. The Thermofax print is shown at right.

SILKSCREEN

Any stamped images or letters can be used in silkscreen printing. Stamp first on paper, correct as needed and modify by enlarging, reducing or collaging. The image can then be used on a photo emulsion silkscreen. The process is somewhat complex but the image can be repeated almost endlessly. Stamped letters were silkscreened in the quilt *Sojourner Truth* (page 42).

LASER TRANS

This special transfer paper allows you to print images from your computer to make decal-like transfers. After scanning in photos and stamped images, words, or letters, the design is printed out on Laser Trans from a color laser printer. The paper is then soaked in water. When the decal slides away from its backing, it will adhere to glass, wood, or fabric. This makes it possible for you to put your stamped images almost anywhere. Laser Trans is a relatively new and versatile product.

COMPUTER

Any stamped image can be scanned into a computer, and altered in dozens of ways. Digital cameras expand the possibilities still further. Once stamped and altered, the images can be scanned and printed onto transfer paper in your ink jet printer or a color laser copier. You can also print directly on fabric, but it will not be permanent unless you use a prepared fabric. See *The Photo Transfer Handbook* for a thorough coverage of those methods.

Judy Schuster uses the computer to develop mock-ups for her tapestries. The sketches she uses to begin the process often include stamps.

Detail of *Spirit: The Heavens, the Earth, Day and Night,* Judy Schuster

Judy starts her work on fabric using stamps, paints, and screen printing. After scanning these into her computer, she selects areas she wants to use, and rotates, crops, and adds color. These are then printed to scale and become the cartoons for her tapestries.

figures: Impress Me

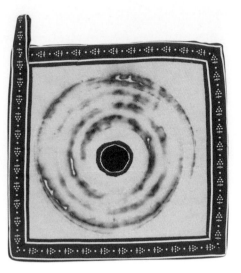

Hot Pot Holder, 8½" x 8½", Ann deWitt

Ann unintentionally stamped her fabric by leaving it on a hot burner. No paints, no stamps required. NOT recommended for any age!

Stir Crazy, 60" x 42½", Sandra Sider, Photo: Karen Bell

The splayed bristles of an old, thick paintbrush served as Sandra's stamp for the entire background of this piece. The Createx "Pearl" Paint varies from strong (and faintly reflective) to dark and subdued. Sandra finds that a small stamp allows her to create subtle background changes. The images of chair, tools, wheels, flowers, and leaves are cyanotype photograms (blueprint) on turquoise cloth.

Dust to Dust, 36" X 36", Sandra Sider, Photo: Karen Bell

The beveled edges of foam brushes were used as stamps to create "bones" on the figure. By altering the angle of the beveled foam, Sandra changes the thickness of the line to create a more interesting pattern. The figure was created by using a cyanotype photogram (blueprint) on magenta cloth. Flowers are photo transferred.

CLOTHING

Few designers, when they are busy with stamps, can resist adding a stamp to whatever they are wearing. It's almost irresistible to stamp a heart on your sleeve, add a green thumb to your garden gloves, or populate a six-year-old's T-shirt with dinosaurs. An incentive for one artist was a drop of paint on her white shirt that (inexplicably) she was wearing as a smock. In covering the drip with a stamp she launched into a whole new world of stamped-clothing design.

An easy way to begin is to use a ready-made garment—a shirt, sweatshirt, socks, boxer shorts, or apron. Something you no longer wear is a perfect target. Stamp it with an all-over pattern, or edge the cuffs and yokes. Or stamp it with animals or faces, add marking-pen balloons (as in comic strips), and invent a conversation for them.

When designing an entire garment, there are two basic approaches: one is to stamp the fabric or yardage from which to cut your pattern, and the other is to cut out pattern parts, then stamp them according to the shapes.

Personalized clothing is always a treat and makes a perfect gift. Even the humble sweatshirt or T-shirt rises to new heights with a favorite quote or a friend's favorite things. Any pet, sport, book, or flower can be a point of departure. If you're making your own stamps, then individualizing is easy—though it's hard to imagine there's an image left that isn't already made into a stamp.

Ancient Sun Spirit: Handbag, 12" x 9", Jane M. Prario

A single stamp is highlighted in the pieced center of this bright-colored tote. The stamped lining matches the vest coat's lining (page 57)

stamps: Impress Me

Handbag #6, 11" x 13", Donna K. Crane

Donna hand-carved E-Z Cut blocks, and stamped onto solid-colored fabrics, as well as fabrics she had already textured. She then cut rectangles or borders around the stamps and machine appliquéd them to the parts of the tote. Donna also used stamped images she carved in a workshop with Natasha Kempers-Cullen.

Back of *Today's Identity,* Susan R. Macy

Susan recycled an old linen jacket—reflecting her identity as she was finishing her doctorate—with the words, "do," "teach," and "study." She filled the borders and edges using whatever stamp fit the space. A single red heart adds contrast.

alphabet: vintage; hearts, checkers, house, asterisk, plants: Jean Ray Laury; spiral, figure: cannot identify

Discharge Flange Jacket, Martie Carroll

Assessing her finished, discharged, cotton sateen jacket, Martie decided to add a leaf stamp for greater interest. The stamp's sharp-edged patterns contrast with the soft-color areas of discharge (page 46). Black Versatex, foam brushed onto her stamp, gives focus to the front panel of the garment.

leaf stamp: Rubber Stampede

Neckties, Lora Wheeler

Stamped and personalized neckties were made for family members at a surprise birthday party. When the ink dried on the silk ties, she added outline or decorative edges with Pilot Metallic Pens.

sun, small sun: Plaid Enterprises Inc.; letters: Simply Stamps; geometric shape, large ethnic motif: Rubber Stampede; bone, dog, hydrant: Stamps for Kids; alphabet: Educational Insights

Child's Shirt, Pele D. Fleming

A friend's daughter did the drawings of these delightful faces, which Pele had custom-made into stamps. Pele prefers to cut out the pattern parts first, stamp her images, and then make the garment.

Tote, 13" x 14", Rosemary Hoffenberg

After hand painting the background colors onto this tote, Rosemary carved her flower stamp design and stamped it using Deka Fabric Paints. Dark green texture and pattern in the background were stamped with an old paint brush.

One-piece T's, Joyce Lytle, Mari Dreyer, Liz Aneloski, Photos: Diane Pedersen

These playful T's were created using a variety of commercial foam stamps and erasers.

stamps: unknown origin

Vest, Sherrill Kahn

Placing a stamp face-up under muslin, Sherrill rubbed it with Crayola® crayons. Washes of applicator-tipped paints went over that, with the crayon providing a resist (page 50) in the fabric. Applicator-tipped paints were used to highlight and outline areas as well as to add new patterns.

all stamps: Impress Me

Back of T-shirt, Kathy Miller

After tracing around a child's foot Kathy cut and discarded the paper feet and ironed the background paper to this T-shirt. She brushed lightly from the edges of the paper towards the center, to outline the shape.

checkerboard: cannot identify; all other stamps: Impress Me

Rainbow Yarn Jacket, Diane Herbort

Diane used yarn lines, appliqué, buttons, and little electronic parts from a radio shop for her jacket. The lining was stamped with commercial stamps as well as kitchen sponges and leaf prints.

geometric shapes: Leavenworth Jackson; running man: Ken Brown; large and small stars, Assyrian Guy: 100 Proof Press; op art squares: Stamp Francisco

Ancient Sun Spirit: Hat Band, Jane M. Prario

Black images stamped on purple encircle the crown of this hat, which is part of an ensemble with her vest coat (page 57).

all stamps: Impress Me

Flannel Hanten Jacket
Martie Carroll

Using a "sponge-on-a-stick," Martie applied Lumiére and Versatex Paints to her flannel, lamé, and marbled cloth. Flannel gives a soft image and lamé creates a reflective now-you-see-it, now-you-don't effect, while the stamping on marbled cloth creates a remarkable complexity of pattern. Machine stitches effectively outline each image.

diagonal line, and big E: Rubber Stampede; spirals: PSX (Personal Stamp Exchange)

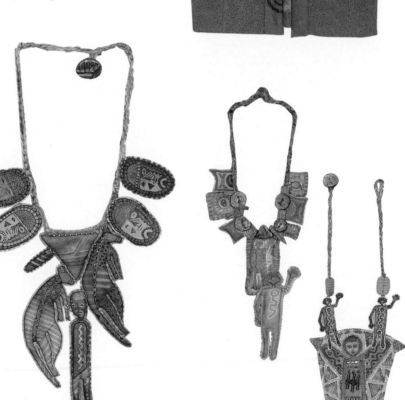

Necklaces with Dolls, 6" to 8" tall, Sherrill Kahn

Stamped and stuffed necklaces demonstrate Sherrill's talent for painting, layering, and embellishing surfaces. Her process is to stamp an image, paint it, and add decorative marking and metallic lines. She then places it right side up with a second layer, sews the two together and trims the edge, allowing about 1/8" of fabric beyond the seam line. Next the figure is stuffed through small slits on the back, using fabric glue to cover the slits. Seam allowances are glued next, and further paint and embellishments are added. She designs her stamps and uses Delta CeramCoat, Dr. Ph. Martin's Ready Tex, and Jacquard Lumiére. The figures are assembled, along with other shapes, and are sewn to braided yarn cords.

stamps: Impress Me

Quilted Jewelry, Pele D. Fleming

Pele stamps her images and colors them with Y&C FabricMate brush-tip markers. She uses a thin batting and backing fabric and very small machine stitches to sew around the edge (as well as within the design). When trimmed, it is ready for the findings, which turn the stuffed pieces into pins, earrings, or decorative additions to hats and clothing.

stamps: Purrfection

Ancient Sun Spirit: Long Vest Coat,
Jane M. Prario

A complex pattern of piecing in the side panels, along with squares and fans on the front, provided Jane with a great range of shapes to stamp within. Whether the shapes were small or large, strips or squares, she found stamps to correspond to the shapes and sizes. Printed fabrics added to the overall complexity. Both the cotton vest and the polyester lining of this remarkable garment are stamped using a make-up sponge with Liquitex Acrylic Fabric Paint. This long vest coat is part of an entire ensemble, including a hat (page 55) and bag (page 53).

stamps: Impress Me; leaf stamp: Inkadinkado®

Silk Scarf, Martie Carroll

After hand painting her silk scarf, Martie stamped it with finely detailed stamps. Nova Color acrylics and metallics were applied along with Flex gel, which adds no color but alters the value of the silk, leaving it silky soft and flexible.

large spiral: PSX (Personal Stamp Exchange); concentric circles: Effie Gletzfinger; words/text: Stampers Anonymous

QUILTS AND WALLHANGINGS

Of all stamping projects, a quilt requires the most sustained effort and attention. Quilt designs vary in complexity, but more traditional ones can be worked in blocks, which simplifies handling. Quiltmakers like handmade stamps because of the large-scale possibilities.

Many of the fabric artists who are into stamping are making wallhangings. Some use stamps as the primary motif of a repeat pattern, as in Elaine Plogman's work (page 62). Others stamp to create textures and patterns for the background. Their versatile use of stamps defies categorizing—many are so integrated into the design that it is visually difficult to determine where the stamping is used. See Maureen Bardusk's work on page 63. We have little sense of its being a stamped quilt—the stamping has been absorbed into the work.

This section includes a range of quilts and wallhangings: humorous, personal, elegant, and commemorative.

Good Golly, Miss Dolly, 32" x 29½", Karen Page

This tribute to Dolly and her cloned counterparts was stamped from a block cut from a drawing of Karen's. By alternating black, white, and gray fabrics and paint, Karen created an entire range of grays. A thinner coat of paint created a different depth of gray than a more opaque one. Directional changes while inking her stamp with the brayer made varying background textures.

The Chocolate Electric, Carrot, Happy Birthday Cake Quilt, 55" x 48", Danita Rafalovich

Angels, roses, clowns, dogs, hearts, kimono-clad women, and carrots combine with dozens of other images to create an explosion of decorative nonsense. The cake itself is a geyser of celebration.

Danita stamped all images in black on white paper. She then photocopied and enlarged the images about 400%. Photo transfers were made of over one hundred images that she transferred (by ironing) to the fabric to create her overall design.

chair, lion: Circus Stamps.; cat with tie, cat with dots, lady in chair, beanie/cat, cat head with party hat, electric cat: Quarter Moon; Albert Einstein, Mona Lisa: Alice in Rubberland; winged heart, confetti, frog, ladybugs, fish: Hero Arts; rose: PSX (Personal Stamp Exchange); three cats, running woman: Stampa Barbara; bi-plane: Stamp in the Hand Co.; spire, Grecian dancer: Leavenworth Jackson; carrots: Crazy Folks; Mickey Mouse: Disney Rubber Stampede; kitten in suit: Beatrix Potter Fredric Warne & Co. for Kidstamps; Tina Turner, climbing cat: cannot identify; standing couple, woman seated, overcoat man, man with hand to forehead, woman swinging from rope: Ken Brown Stamps; cat face, sunglasses pig: All Night Media, Inc.; 20s dancer, standing couple, woman pointing right: Fruit Basket Upset; window, naked woman: Rubber Stamps of America; tub: Rubber Stamp Works; fabric bolts: The Happy Stamps; woman in glasses: Raw Stamps; cat with glasses: Daneland for Rubberland; three Alice in Wonderland stamps: Alice in Rubberland; cake: Rubber Buggy Baby Bumpers; Bud: Bizzaro; light: Neato Stuff; leaping lady: Emerald City

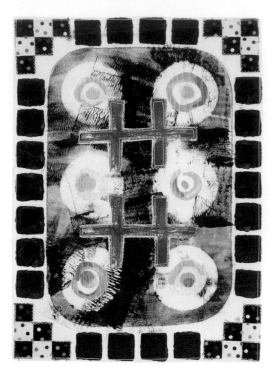

Small Textures Series #2, 13¹/₂" x 9³/₄",
Jeanne Williamson

Jeanne used a combination of rubber gum erasers
and monoprinting. Commercially-printed fabrics
were appliquéd over the background area. She
quilted in straight, parallel, and zigzag stitches.

Solitude, 58" x 43", Rosemary Hoffenberg,
Photo: David Caras

Along with screen printing, Rosemary stamped
with a hand-cut lineoleum block, a sea sponge,
coral, and a wood scrap. Over the mono-printed,
pieced circle she stamped in blue with a
potato masher.

Sweet Love, 29¹/₂" x 57", Therese May

The exuberance of Therese's triptych results from her determination to embellish every square inch! She first appliqués her
fabrics, using both straight and satin stitches, letting all threads dangle. Her stamps, made from sheet rubber mounted on wood
blocks, are printed with acrylic over everything. Buttons, beads, thread, jewels, and painted patterns embellish the love-struck
teapot, the adored teacup, and the rest of the three panels.

American Pie, 30" x 50", Karen Felicity Berkenfeld

Birds carved from E-Z Cut Blocks are stamped over pieced fabrics from old men's shirts. (Karen says the shirts, not the men, are old.) Flexicut is mounted on Plexiglas to make stamps for the highway. She made Styrofoam shapes to stamp the light blue of the trucks, adding details with a linoleum block. Karen makes abundant use of stamps and wipe-out tools (page 34) and enriches every piece of fabric within her reach.

Detail of *Shoe the Blues Away,* Marsha J. Burdick

Shoe stamps inspired Marsha to express her passion for footwear. Even the Flying Geese border sports shoes are stamped with fabric ink. Marsha's common sense advice includes "Bad hairday? Buy new shoes!" "Didn't win the lottery? Buy new shoes!" Shoes at center are appliqued; corner shoes are thermofaxed (page 51) designs from a magnet set.

spectator pump: Bizzaro; clog: Graven Images; polka dot heel: Rubber Man; platform heel: Stamp Francisco

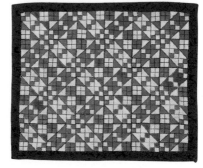

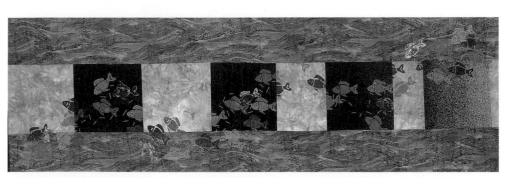

Lure, 35" x 67", Ingrid Law

Using a single stamp, Ingrid created an entire school of fish. Some head upstream over ever-deepening pieced colors and water-patterned fabric. Lightly foiled fish and gold embroidered lines mingle with green metallic machine quilting.

fish: CHUNKY STAMPS

Houses, 7" x 5½"; *Barn Raising,* 6½" x 6½"; *Underground Railroad,* 5½" x 6", Pele D. Fleming

Miniature quilts from Pele's custom-made stamps were colored with permanent markers.

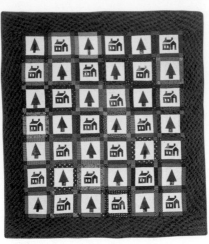

Houses in the Forest, 52" x 47", Carol Olson

The house and tree, cut from Flexi-Foam, are examples of the simple forms Carol recommends for her beginning students.

Acorns and Oak Leaves, 15" x 15", by Paula Peargin

In her first quilt, made in a class with Carol Oslon, Paula used a 5" muslin square, within which she stamped the acorn and leaves. Versatex paints in different thicknesses, applied with a foam brush give dark and light changes to the repeated pattern.

fat sumo wrestler: cannot identify, self-mounted; thin sumo wrestlers reaching to left: Alice in Rubberland; kitten, cat: cannot identify, self-mounted; ferns: Leavenworth Jackson; light bulb: Gumball Graphics; hanging light: Neato Stuff; rose: PSX (Personal Stamp Exchange); "Departed" button: Tin Can Post; stars, confetti: Hero Arts; small chick, small rockets, stars, cats and scroll design: A.N.T. Transfer; two women visiting: Quarter Moon; animals in sunglasses: All Night Media, Inc.; man in sunglasses: Zeitology

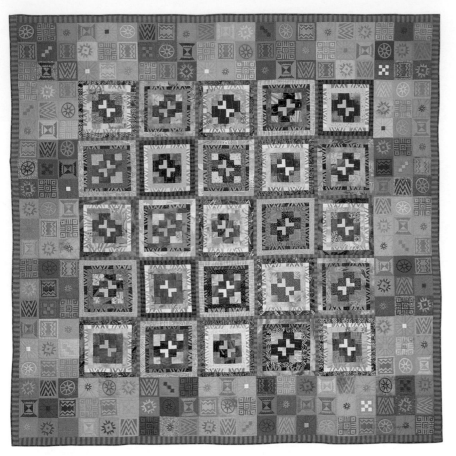

Hopscotch Heaven, 65" x 65", Elaine Plogman

Elaine's collection of handmade 3" x 3" stamps, carved from Speedy Cut, were the inspiration for this quilt. Most of her stamp patterns are original, though some are adapted from a Dover book on African designs.

Wherever You Go, There You Are, 18½" x 17½", Danita Rafalovich

In the center of this piece Danita has composed a scene—sumo wrestlers astride lightbulbs or walking tightropes. Stamps used in the borders are repeated patterns, like quilt blocks.

Evening Tea, 14" x 15½",
Marsha J. Burdick

Leaves sponged with Lumiére paint and stamped onto black fabric were machine quilted at the edge to define the shapes. The geometric Gordian Knot designs, also sponged, are from an old wood block from India. The panel was started in a class with Sherrill Kahn.

Japan Cube #1: Judy Kins

Textures, Maps and Grids #5, 52" x 34",
Jeanne Williamson

The bright colored discs, at center, and the green grids were stamped from Jeanne's carved gum erasers. Maps, cut into segments, are photo transfer. Hand painting and bright-hued quilting threads add to the patterns and textures of this wholecloth quilt.

Wallhanging, 24" x 14½", Sherrill Kahn

After stamping designs with acryic, Sherrill added color washes of Dr. Ph. Martin's Ready Tex over the resist. Paint in applicator-tipped bottles was used to highlight shapes, adding detail and complexity.

stamps: Impress Me by Sherrill Kahn

Stratum, 31" x 41", Maureen Bardusk

In the background, Maureen's wipeout (page 34) patterns create a rich texture over which layers of stamping, collage, piecing, and quilting are added. Using art gum erasers and linoleum blocks, she stamps with Jacquard Textile Paints, Liquitex metallics, and non-metallic acrylics. The surface is overlaid with annealed copper, heavy satin, plastic metallic mesh, and quilting.

1995 the Year of the Boar, 45" x 36", Lisa Gray Hollerbach

After creating her background fabrics by discharging and hand painting, Lisa proceeded to print with her handmade stamp depicting a ram's head. Additional texture was added by stamping with a kitchen whisk. The solid, dark pig was made with a contact paper stencil. The contact paper was applied to the black fabric and discharge (page 46) was used over it to bleach the background. The boar stamp, shown on the right was stamped in black. Another stamp made from Fun Foam was used for metallics and fluorescents.

Back detail of *1995 the Year of the Boar,*
Lisa Gray Hollerbach

This boar stamp design came from a bacon press that Lisa traced and reduced in size on a photocopy machine. She then drew it onto Scratch-Foam® Board, used a spoon to scoop away the excess background foam, and added the lines with a pencil. The foam was then mounted on an adhesive-backed vinyl flooring tile and the excess tile was cut away.

The Little Heart Thief, 11" x 18", Diane Herbort

Stamped fabrics are interspersed with prints, lace, photo transfer, embroidery, and edgings in this fanciful Valentine. Diane added satin hearts, striped binding, buttons, charms, and bugle beads.

red lips: Inkadinkadoo; hearts: Museum of Modern Rubber

Gecko Morning, 49" x 39", Katy Jane Widger

Katy's hand-carved linoleum block is surrounded by triangles of her hand-dyed fabrics. The gecko was reproduced for her line of stamps. Other stamps are carved from potatoes or wood blocks.

Supplication, 76" x 54", Natasha Kempers-Cullen, Photo: Dennis Griggs

Numerous hand-carved E-Z Cut blocks stamped their way into this collaged piece. A plastic strawberry basket was used as a stamp to create the red grid along the right-hand side.

Collage Soup, 59" x 59½", Natasha Kempers-Cullen with Alice May Brock, Photo: Dennis Griggs

The energetic and complex patterns of this collaged quilt resulted from the pooled efforts of Natasha and Alice May Brock (of Alice's Restaurant). Created for *Women of Taste: An Artists and Chefs Collaboration,* they found parallels between collage and soup-making. Stamped and printed words and images fill the background. Bowls at the bottom were cut from fabric printed with antique batik blocks. Other collaged shapes were cut from densely stamped or screened fabric, then over-painted.

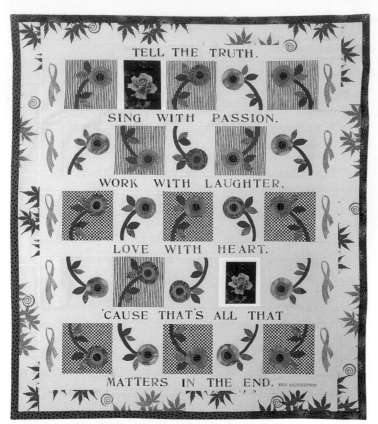

To My Dear Mama, 50" x 41", Kata Patton

On the fifth anniversary of her mother's death from breast cancer, Kata finished this personal tribute. Her mother's love of roses inspired the photo transfers. Maple leaves in the border were silkscreen printed, while the pink ribbons were hand carved from Safety-Kut.

spiral: CHUNKY STAMPS; alphabet: Standard Rubber Type Co., Ltd.

Hearts Quilt, 48" x 40", Carol Olson

A 7" Flexi-Foam heart was mounted on the bottom of a Pyrex casserole dish, so Carol could see through it for easy placement on the block. Smaller stamps were used over the heart in a darker color after the first layer dried and was heat-set.

small star, small spiral, thick spiral, hearts: Simply Stamps; largest spiral, thin spiral: Rubber Stampede; star: Stamp Affair

Sunny Delight, 21½" x 19", Arlene Kovash

Arlene randomly stamped suns over the fabric using Jacquard Textile Paint in golds and yellows. Then she cut squares from the stamped muslin, joined the squares, cut out the borders (stamped with stars), and assembled the parts. Last, she added several stars to overlap seam lines.

three suns: Good Stamps Stampgoods; sun: Posh Impressions; sun: Quarter Moon; sun: Asya Graphics; sun: unidentified; star: PSX (Personal Stamp Exchange)

AROUND THE HOUSE

CHAPTER 7

Stamping offers a way to individualize the stuff of everyday use. Napkins, pillowcases, aprons, and sheets are ready to go, just waiting for you to wave a stamp in their direction. Children love seeing their names on personal belongings, and that is easily accomplished with stamps.

Homes are full of fabric things that seem irresistible to the dedicated stamper. I like working on dishtowels; they are inexpensive, ready-made, all cotton, usable things that don't have to fit anybody and the colors don't have to match. Personalizing is easy and stamped messages are a natural.

Start with some easy-to-do ready-mades. After a few successes you will be ready to stamp anything you can get your paint-covered hands on.

Red and Yellow Pillow, Jean Ray Laury

Stamps for these pillows were scissor-cut from 1/4"-thick PenScore, and rubber cemented to a 1/2"-thick PenScore block, then stamped with Versatex. They are sewn, assembled, and quilted like the pillows in the project on page 70.

Stuffed Cat, 9" tall, Kata Patton

Kata stamped her words and designs on muslin strips, then machine stitched the strips to the front, inserting a decorative edging. For the eyes, stamped stars were given sequin centers. The face was embroidered and the parts were then assembled and stuffed. She hand carved her hearts, as well as the letters, which came from a copyright-free alphabet.

Computer Mouse Pad, Adrianne N. A. Shroyer, Photo: Diane Pedersen

Adrianne stamped this mousepad using Fun to Paint® Dotters by Plaid® Enterprises, from the craft store.

Jester, 16" x 16", Kata Patton

Kata made stamps for the face: two for the eyes, one for the nose, and one for the pouty mouth. The pillow is from a 1987 Simplicity pattern.

Dish Towel, Kathy Miller

Kathy traced her hand on freezer paper, cut out the shape and tossed the "hand" away. She then ironed the background shape onto fabric, and sponge printed within the open areas, and stamped within it.

all stamps: Impress Me

Priority Mail, 7½" x 8½", Karen Page

After cutting her envelopes from 70-weight canvas, Karen painted them. She used her sewing machine like a drawing tool and added handmade paper, fabric fragments and permanent marker details.

alphabet: Ivory Coast; bird: The Herbarium

Napkins, 8" x 4", Juliana Alspaugh

Many of the leaves and petals Juliana uses for printing were first dried and pressed in an old book. They are easily inked, placed face down on fabric, covered, and pressed lightly with the fingers.

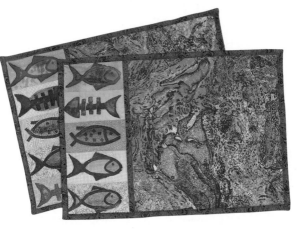

Fish Placemats, 12½" x 17", Susan L. Smeltzer

Weatherstripping in varying widths, mounted on Plexiglas, was used to make these fish stamps. After stamping and heat-setting the bold outline of the fish, Susan painted in the open areas.

Cabbage Placemat, 12½" x 17", Jean Ray Laury

Cabbages were stamped on green and yellow fabric, dried, heat-set, then hand tinted with Versatex thinned to a water-color consistency, and pieced.

cabbage: Rubber Stampede

Crib Set: Pillow 8¾" x 16¾", Sheet 58" x 45", Jean Ray Laury

Sponge alphabet stamps were used to print this crib set. Use a ready-made sheet and pillowcase or make your own—also great idea for larger bed-sizes.

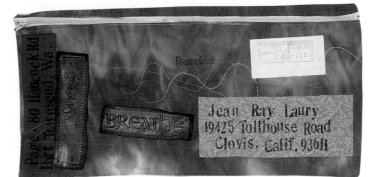

Sachets, 6" x 2", Kata Patton

Small cloth bags filled with lavender are perfect projects for the beginning stamper. Kata used muslin and small-scale prints that allow the words to be easily read.

Mailer, 7" x 14", Karen Page

Hand painting and machine stitching were used to color and decorate the heavy cotton of this envelope. Leather-like pieces were created when Karen heated scraps of Flexi-Foam with an embossing heat gun until they were soft enough to impress with a stamp, and then rubbed them with metallic color. After adding the "leather" pieces, she assembled the envelope, zipped it shut, and sent it to me.

letters: old alphabet sets; word: ERA Graphics; figure: Acey Deucy

Envelopes, Karen Page

Hand-dyed and marbleized fabrics cut for envelopes were stamped and edged with varigated zigzag stitches. The folded-in sides were overlapped by the bottom fold and the edges were secured with double-faced adhesive fabric.

fish: Red Pearl; joy: Judi Kims; woman: handmade by Susan Longerse; cat: Purrfection; foot print: All Night Media

Hydrangea Pillow, 16" x 16", Juliana Alspaugh

While it is easier to handle and make multiple prints from a dried leaf, Juliana used fresh ones for this pillow. She applies her block printing ink to either side of the leaf using a foam pad and places it on her pre-washed fabric. A piece of newsprint goes over that, and she gently presses the leaf or petal.

SPIRAL PILLOWS

14" x 14", Jean Ray Laury

SUPPLIES

Contrasting fabrics: one 5" x 5" square of each of four colors for the center

Background fabric: one 15" x 15" square for pillow front and one 14½" x 14½" square for the pillow back

Muslin: 18" x 18"

Batting: 18" x 18"

Pillow form: 14"

³⁄₈"-wide weatherstripping insulation tape: 14"

3" diameter drinking glass or 3" square of Plexiglas for the stamp base

Fabric paint or ink

STAMPING

MAKING THE STAMP

Following the spiral pattern, place the weatherstripping sticky side down on the bottom of the drinking glass or Plexiglas block. Trim off any excess length of weatherstripping.

Spiral Pattern

PRINTING WITH THE STAMP

Print the stamp onto the 5" fabric squares. Heat-set if necessary following the manufacturer's instructions.

Stamp spiral onto square.

PILLOW CONSTRUCTION

PILLOW CENTER

Use ¼" seam allowance.

1. Trim the stamped squares to 4" x 4", centering the design. You should have about ½" between the edge of the design and the edges of the fabric.

2. Arrange the squares.

3. Stitch two of the squares together. Press the seam allowances to one side. Repeat for the other two squares. *If you press the seams with the seam allowances facing in opposite directions the center of the pillow will line up perfectly.* Stitch the pairs together. Press the seam to one side.

Stitch pairs, then stitch the pairs together.

4. Press raw edge under ¼" on the outside edge.

5. Choosing either a diagonal (on-point) or straight orientation, center the stamped squares onto the 15" pillow front and topstitch close to the outside edge.

Pillow center on pillow front; straight

*Pillow center on pillow front;
diagonally (on-point)*

6. Layer and baste the pillow top, batting, and muslin following the general instructions (pages 90-91).

7. Quilt around each stamped design.

8. Quilt the unstamped background area of the pillow top with straight lines or spirals.

> TIP: *To use the stamp to mark the quilting design: dip the thoroughly clean stamp in water, tap it lightly onto a paper towel, and then tap it more firmly on the background fabric. Quilt around the edge of the wet design. By the time the quilting is finished the fabric will be nearly dry.*

PILLOW FINISHING

1. Trim the pillow front to 14½" x 14½".

2. Place the pillow front and back with right sides together and stitch around the outside edge, leaving a 10" opening on one side to insert the pillow form. Trim the corner seam allowances.

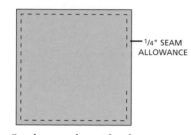

¼" SEAM ALLOWANCE

Stitch around outside edge leaving 10" opening. Trim.

3. Turn right-side out and insert the pillow form. Slipstitch the opening closed.

FLYING GEESE PLACEMAT

12½" x 16", Susan L. Smeltzer

SUPPLIES

Yardage amounts are based on 42" fabric width. Supplies and instructions are for one placemat.

Various fabrics: one 5" x 3" rectangle from each of six colors for the large flying geese triangles

Background fabric: 1/8 yard for the small flying geese triangles

Main fabric: one 11 1/2" x 12 1/2" rectangle for the large section

Accent stripe: 1/4 yard for accent strip and binding

Backing: 16" x 20"

Batting: 16" x 20"

Stamp

Fabric paint or ink

CUTTING

Background fabric:
Cut twelve 2 1/2" x 2 1/2" squares.

Accent stripe:
Cut one 1" x 12 1/2" strip.

Binding:
Cut two strips 2 1/2" x width of fabric.

STAMPING

Stamp your choice of designs onto the 5" x 3" rectangles. Let the design overlap the bottom edge and make sure the design is centered from side to side. Heat-set if necessary, following the manufacturer's instructions.

FLYING GEESE CONSTRUCTION

Use 1/4" seam allowance.

1. Trim the stamped rectangles to 4 1/2" x 2 1/2", centering the design.

2. Fold the 2 1/2" background squares in half diagonally. Fingerpress to make a slight crease to mark the diagonal line on each square.

3. Align the corner of one square with one corner of a stamped rectangle.

4. Stitch on the crease of the fold from corner to corner. Trim away excess fabric from underneath corner.

5. Press the seam allowances toward the background triangle.

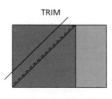

Align corners, stitch on fold, and trim.

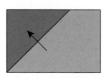

Press.

6. Complete the second side and press. Repeat for all six rectangles.

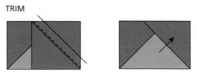

Repeat for other side.

PLACEMAT CONSTRUCTION

1. Stitch the six flying geese into one vertical section. Press. It should measure 12½" x 4½".

2. Stitch the accent strip to the right-hand side of the flying geese section. Press.

3. Stitch the 12½" side of the main placemat fabric to the other side of the accent strip. Press.

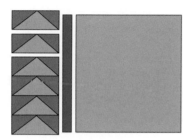

Placemat Construction

PLACEMAT FINISHING

1. Layer and baste following the general instructions (pages 90-91).

2. Quilt along the seam lines, stitching in the ditch. Mark quilt lines on the main fabric with a chalk pencil or other quilt marker and quilt.

3. Trim the edges even and square.

4. Bind following the general instructions (page 91).

Alternate Color Schemes

ENVELOPES

Jean Ray Laury

small hands: old alphabet set;
large hand: CHUNKY STAMPS

letters: old alphabet set

letters: old office stamp set;
trees: Posh Impressions;
chicken: unknown origin

These envelopes can be delivered through the United States Postal Service. Be sure to add a secure closure—this can be a snap, velcro, a ribbon tie, long running stitches in a contrasting color, or anything else you can think of.

SUPPLIES

Envelope #1: Happy Birthday (great for inserting $$$)
Envelope #2: Heart & Hand
Envelope #3: Chickens and Trees

Envelope #1: Two contrasting fabrics: one 7¹/2" x 12" rectangle from each of two fabrics

Envelope #2: One 9" x 12" rectangle from each of two fabrics

Envelope #3: One 10¹/4" x 8³/4" rectangle and one 10¹/4" x 13" rectangle from each of two contrasting fabrics, and one 10¹/4" x 4³/4" rectangle from a third contrasting fabric

Fusible adhesive: 7¹/2" x 12" for Envelope #1 and 9" x 12" for Envelope #2 (not needed for Envelope #3); scraps for address labels (optional)

Ribbon: 31" (optional)

Stamps

Fabric paint or ink

ENVELOPE #1 AND #2 CONSTRUCTION

1. Place the two contrasting fabrics, wrong sides together, with the fusible adhesive between the two fabric layers. Fuse following the manufacturer's instructions.

2. Trim Envelope #1 to 6 ³/4" x 11" or Envelope #2 to 8" x 11". Trim the envelope flap following the pattern. Use the pattern to mark the cutting lines for the envelope flap. Cut on the marked line.

3. Stamp the envelope. Test by folding to make sure the designs will appear right side up. Heat-set if necessary.

4. Zigzag stitch around the raw edges if desired.

5. Fold the bottom edge up and press.

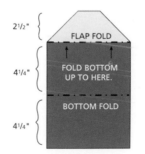

Happy Birthday Envelope #1

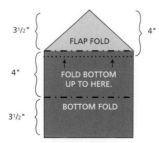

Heart & Hand Envelope #2

6. Use either a straight or zigzag stitch and stitch 1/8" from the edge through all layers; starting at bottom edge, continue around the envelope flap, and down the other side.

7. Write or stamp the address on a contrasting color, then fuse to the front of the envelope using fusible adhesive.

Optional: Attach a ribbon to the front of the envelope as a closure.

ENVELOPE #3 CONSTRUCTION

1. With right sides together, stitch the small-and medium-sized rectangles together along the 10¼" side and press.

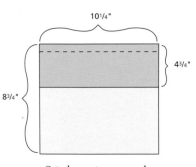

10¼"

4¾"

8¾"

Stitch sections together.

2. Place the pieced fabric created in step 1, wrong sides together with the large rectangle. Trim the envelope flap following the pattern.

3. Stamp your choice of designs onto the envelope. Test by folding to make sure the designs will appear right side up. Heat-set if necessary following the manufacturer's instructions.

4. Place right sides together and stitch using 1/8" seam allowance,

leaving an opening in the middle of one edge. Turn right side out and press.

WRONG SIDE

Stitch leaving an opening on one edge.

5. Fold the bottom edge up and press.

6. Topstitch 1/8" from the edge through all layers; stitch down the right-hand side, across the bottom, and up the left-hand side. Be sure to catch the opening left for turning.

RIGHT SIDE

Top stitch 1/8" from the edge.

7. Add a ribbon, snap, button and loop, or velcro dots to seal the envelope closed.

8. Write or stamp address on a contrasting color, then adhere to front of envelope using fusible adhesive.

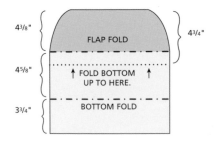

4⅜"

FLAP FOLD

4¾"

4⅝"

↑ FOLD BOTTOM UP TO HERE. ↑

3¾"

BOTTOM FOLD

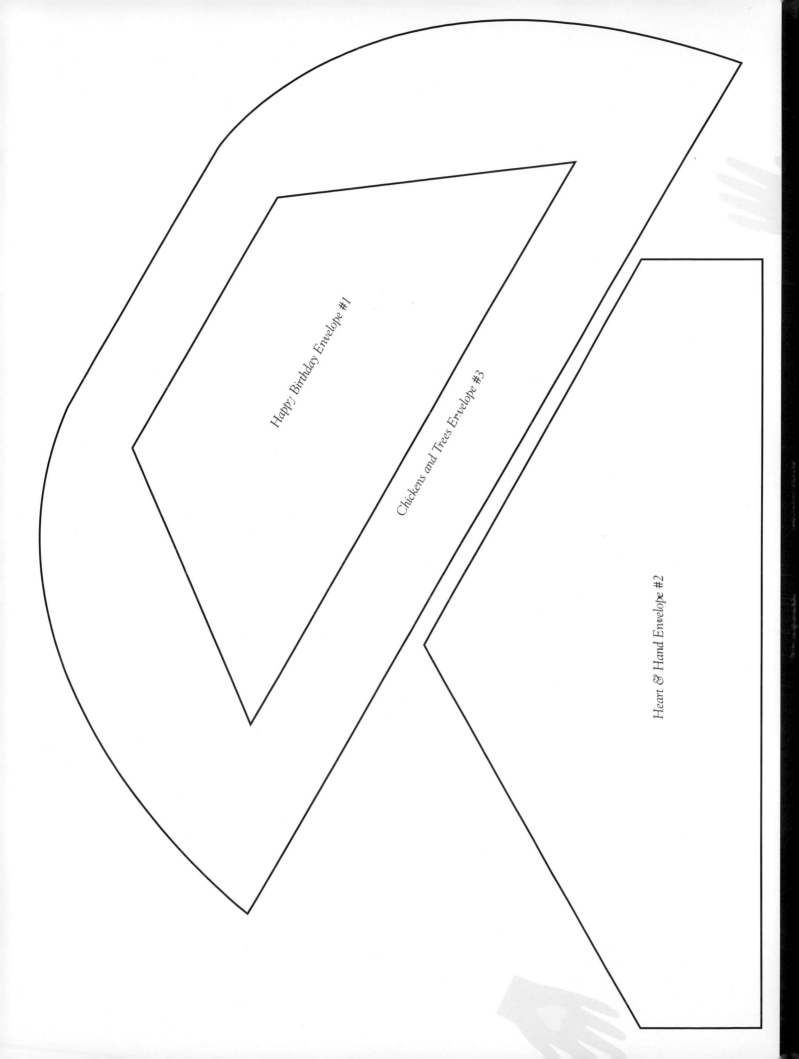

Happy Birthday Envelope #1

Chickens and Trees Envelope #3

Heart & Hand Envelope #2

CHILD'S QUILT

32$\frac{1}{2}$" x 38", Carol Olson

spiral and sun: CHUNKY STAMPS

SUPPLIES

Yardage amounts are based on 42"
fabric width.

White: 3/4 yard for the background squares

Bright fabrics: 1/2 yard total of a variety of fabrics for the sashing strips and cornerstones

Magenta: 3/4 yard for the borders

Backing: 1 yard

Batting: 36" x 42"

Binding: 3/8 yard

Stamps

Fabric paint or ink

CUTTING

White:
Cut twenty 6" x 6" squares.

Bright fabrics:
Cut forty-nine 1 1/2" x 5" strips for the sashing strips.

Cut thirty 1 1/2" x 1 1/2" squares for the sashing cornerstones.

Magenta:
Cut two 5" x 29" strips for the side borders.

Cut two 5" x 32 1/2" strips for the top and bottom borders.

Binding:
Cut four strips 2 1/2" x width of fabric

STAMPING

Stamp your choice of designs onto the white squares. Heat-set if necessary following the manufacturer's instructions.

QUILT CONSTRUCTION

Use 1/4" seam allowance.

1. Trim the blocks to 5" x 5", centering the design.

2. Lay out the blocks, sashing, and cornerstones. Be sure to avoid placing fabrics that match next to each other.

3. Sew into horizontal rows. Press the seam allowances of the first row to the right, the second row to the left, and so on.

4. Sew the rows together matching the sashing strip and cornerstone seams. Press.

5. Add the borders to the sides of the quilt top and then to top and bottom.

Quilt Top Construction

6. Layer and baste following the general instructions (pages 90-91).

7. Quilt as desired.

8. Bind following the general instructions (page 91).

CHERRIES QUILT

42" x 42", Jean Ray Laury

To ensure clear and even stamping choose a tightly woven fabric with a smooth surface.

SUPPLIES

Yardage amounts are based on 42" fabric width.

White: 1³/4 yards for blocks and borders

Red: ¹/3 yard for sashing

Backing: 1¹/2 yards

Batting: 45" x 45"

Binding: ¹/2 yard

Stamps:

Large ring for wreath: ³/8"-wide weatherstripping adhered to an 8" plastic disc that came with a bakery cake

Medium circle (cherry) and two leaves: cut art gum erasers

Tulip, tulip leaves, and flower: scissor-cut Sticky-Back Flexi-Foam adhered to ¹/2"-thick PenScore.

Scallop and corner scallop: cut ³/8"-thick PenScore adhered to Plexiglas

Stem: ¹/2"-wide weatherstripping adhered to ¹/2" or ³/8" PenScore

Large circle for flower: stiff foam puzzle part

Large dot: end of a foam brush

Small dot: pencil eraser

Fabric paint or ink

CUTTING

White:

Cut four 15" x 15" squares for the center blocks.

Cut four 6¹/4" x 30¹/2" strips for the borders.

Cut four 6¹/4" x 6¹/4" squares for the border corners.

Red:

Cut six 1¹/2" x 14" strips for the vertical sashing.

Cut three 1¹/2" x 30¹/2" strips for the horizontal sashing.

Turquoise:

Cut four strips 2¹/2" x width of fabric. (Cut five strips if your fabric width is less than 44".)

STAMPING

1. Practice on a leftover piece of white fabric.

2. Choose one or all four of the block designs. Repeating one design four times will make a wonderful quilt (and use fewer stamps). Make your stamps following directions beginning on page 11 and using the patterns provided on page 85.

3. Fold the large center squares both vertically and horizontally and make slight creases to mark the center and to help stamp placement. Follow directions on page 35 for registration (alignment).

4. Refer to the photograph for stamp placement. Stamp the large circles for the wreaths first. Then stamp the stems that are in

the four corners, or the cherries at the top, bottom, and sides to help keep the design symmetrical. Finish stamping the rest of the shapes.

5. Fold each border strip in half lengthwise twice to divide the border into four sections.

6. Stamp the scallops first. Then stamp the cherries and leaves in the centers of the scallops to help keep the design symmetrical. Finish stamping the rest of the shapes.

7. Fold the border corner squares both vertically and horizontally and make slight creases to mark the center and help pattern placement.

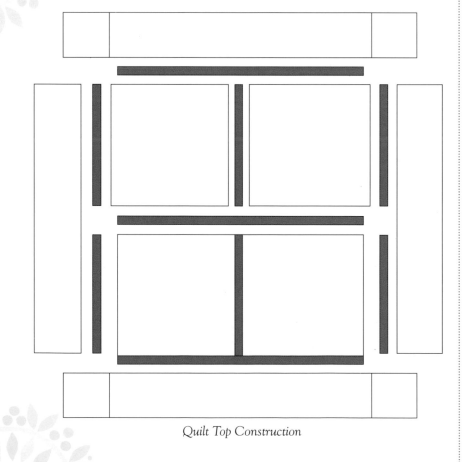

Quilt Top Construction

8. Stamp the shapes.

9. Heat-set if necessary following the manufacturer's instructions.

QUILT CONSTRUCTION

Use ¹/4" seam allowance.

1. Trim the large center blocks to 14" x 14", centering the design.

2. Lay out the blocks and sashing strips.

3. Sew into horizontal rows. Press the seam allowances toward the sashing.

4. Sew the rows together with horizontal sashing between the rows, aligning the vertical sashing strips. Then sew a horizontal sashing strip to the top and bottom.

5. Add the two side border strips to the sides of the quilt top. Stitch a border corner to each end of the remaining two border strips and add to the top and bottom of the quilt top.

6. Layer and baste following the general instructions (pages 90-91).

7. Quilt as desired. I quilted by stitching the outlines of the stamps, then a ¹/2" grid in the center of the wreaths, and ³/8" outline stitches echoing the patterns to fill in the rest.

8. Bind following the general instruction (page 91).

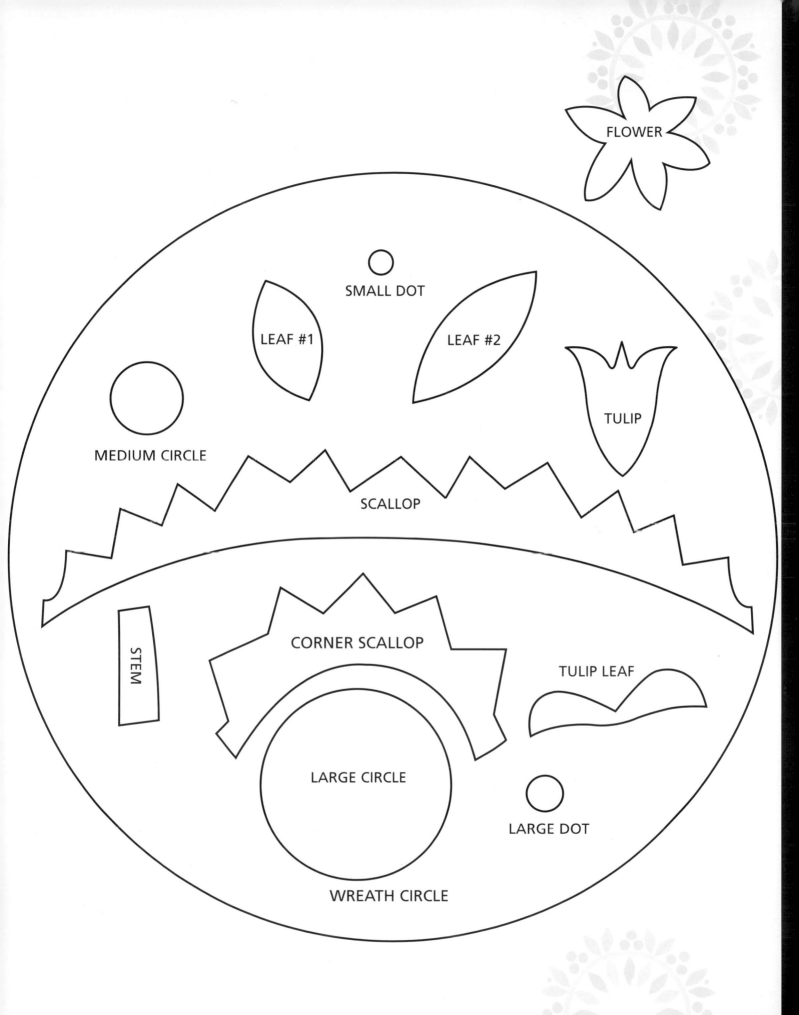

FLOWER

SMALL DOT

LEAF #1

LEAF #2

TULIP

MEDIUM CIRCLE

SCALLOP

STEM

CORNER SCALLOP

TULIP LEAF

LARGE CIRCLE

LARGE DOT

WREATH CIRCLE

STAMPED DRUNKARD'S PATH QUILT

48$\frac{1}{2}$" x 60$\frac{1}{2}$", Liz Aneloski

SUPPLIES

*Yardage amounts are based on 42"
fabric width.*

*Fabric Hint: Pick a fabric you love
that includes several colors. Let these
colors guide you in choosing the other
fabrics. Use this fabric as one of your
fabric choices.*

Light- to medium-colored fabrics:
1/4 yard each of 26 different fabrics
(13 pairs of fabrics) for the 48
center blocks

Medium- to dark-colored fabrics:
1/4 yard each of 16 different fabrics
for the 32 border blocks and binding

Backing: 3 yards

Batting: 52" x 64"

Magic-Rub and pencil-top erasers

Opaque white fabric paint

CUTTING

Light- to medium-colored fabrics:
Cut 2 using template A and 2
using template B from each fabric
for the center section.

Medium- to dark-colored fabrics:
Cut 2 using template A and 2
using template B from each fabric
for the border.

Cut 2 1/2"-wide strips from the leftover fabrics for the binding. Piece
into one length approximately 240".

BLOCKS FOR CENTER SECTION

Use 1/4" seam allowance.

*You will have enough pieces to make 52
blocks (4 blocks from each of the fabric
pairs). After laying out the blocks, use
the extra blocks to practice stamping.*

1. Referring to the photograph,
   arrange the pairs of fabrics until
   you are happy with the balance
   of light and medium, calm and
   busy. *Note: Notice how the blocks
   containing the pairs of fabrics are
   kept together, and that you will use
   three blocks of some pairs of fabrics
   and four blocks of other pairs.*

2. Pick up the two pieces for one of
   the blocks. Fingerpress a crease in
   the center of the curved side of
   each piece. Pin with right sides
   together (A on top), along the
   curved edge, matching the ends
   and centers. Continue pinning
   the rest of the curve.

Pin with A on top.

3. Stitch (A on top) and press
   toward B. Repeat steps 1-3 to
   make 52 blocks.

Stitch with A on top.

Drunkard's Path Block

4. Stitch the blocks into horizontal rows. Press the seam allowances of the first row to the right, the second row to the left, and so on.

5. Stitch the rows together. Press.

BLOCKS FOR BORDERS

1. Pair the cut A and B pieces randomly and arrange them around the center section until you are happy with the balance of medium and dark, calm and busy.

2. Repeat steps 1-3 above to make 32 border blocks.

Quilt Top Construction

3. Stitch the 8 blocks for one of the side borders in a row. Press. Add to one side of the center section. Repeat for the other side.

4. Repeat for the top and bottom borders.

STAMPING

1. Make a paper pattern of the finished size of piece A (the dashed line). Mark the stamp alignment lines on the pattern.

2. Using the pattern and the short side of the Magic Rub eraser, stamp the design on B, aligning the eraser with the lines on the pattern.

3. Stamp the dots on A with the pencil-top eraser; spacing the dots evenly. Heat-set if necessary following the manufacturer's instructions.

FINISHING

1. Layer and baste following the general instructions (pages 90-91).

2. Quilt in-the-ditch between the blocks and following the curve of the stamped design.

3. Bind following the general instructions (page 91).

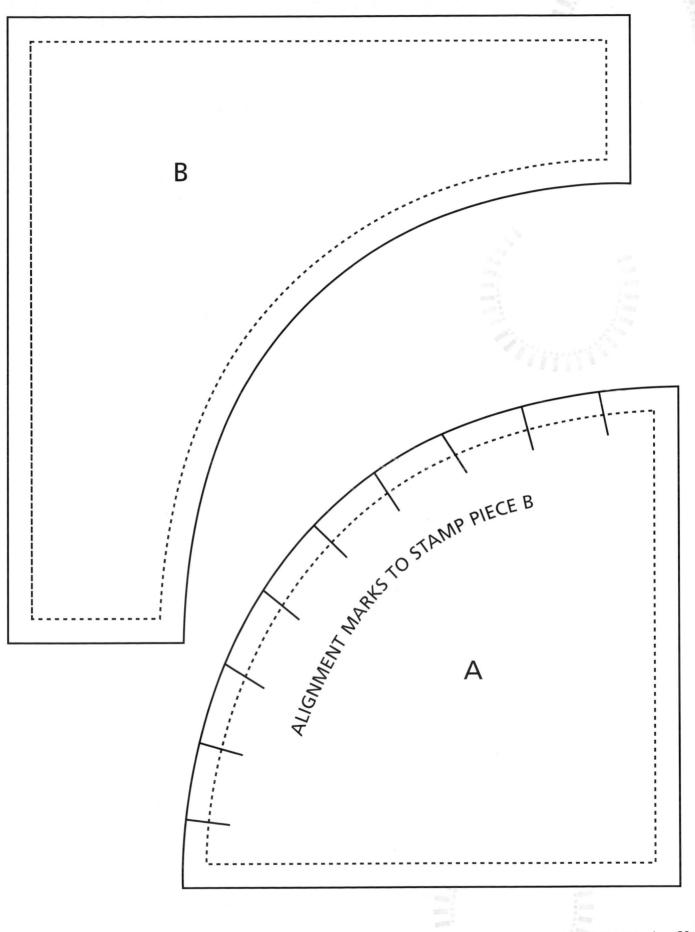

B

ALIGNMENT MARKS TO STAMP PIECE B

A

SEWING BASICS

SUPPLIES

Basic sewing supplies

Sewing machine: In good working order (We recommend starting any new project with a new needle.)

Template plastic

Rotary cutting ruler

Rotary cutter and mat

Fabric: Use 100% cotton for the quilts. We recommend pre-washing all of your fabric, especially if you are planning to make a quilt that will require laundering.

Fabric requirements are based on a 42" width; many fabrics shrink when washed, and widths vary by manufacturer. In the cutting instructions, strips are generally cut on the crosswise grain.

SEWING BASICS

SEAM ALLOWANCES

Use 1/4" for all pieced projects, unless told otherwise. It's a good idea to do a test seam before you begin sewing to check that your 1/4" is accurate.

PRESSING

In general, press seams toward the darker fabric. Press lightly in an up-and-down motion. Avoid using a very hot iron or over-ironing, which can distort shapes and blocks.

BORDERS

When measurements are given for border strips to be cut on the crosswise grain, diagonally piece the strips together to achieve the needed lengths.

1. Place pins at the centers of all four sides of the quilt top, and do the same with each side border strip.

2. Pin the borders to the quilt top matching the center pins and corner edges.

3. Using a 1/4" seam allowance, sew the borders to the quilt top in the order given in the project instructions and press.

BACKING

Use 100% cotton for the backing of the quilts. Plan on making the backing a minimum of 2" larger than the quilt top on all sides. Pre-wash the fabric, and trim the selvages before you piece.

To economize, you can piece the back from any leftover fabrics or blocks in your collection. Backing yardages are based on the diagrams.

BATTING

The type of batting to use is a personal decision; for a more traditional look consider using a very thin cotton batting, and then washing the quilt after you have finished quilting it. Some cotton battings can be bought by the yard; consult your local quilt shop. Cut batting approximately 2" larger on all sides than your quilt top.

LAYERING

1. Spread the backing wrong side up and tape the edges down with masking tape. (If you are working on carpet you can use T-pins to secure the backing to the carpet.)

2. Center the batting on top, smooth out any folds. Place the quilt top right side up on top of the batting and backing, making sure it's centered.

BASTING

If you plan to machine quilt, pin baste the quilt layers together with safety pins placed every 3" to 4" apart. Begin basting in the center and move toward the edges first in vertical, then horizontal, rows.

If you plan to hand quilt, baste the layers together with thread using a long needle and light-colored thread. Knot one end of the thread. Using stitches approximately the length of the needle, begin in the center and move out toward the edges.

QUILTING

Quilting enhances the design of the quilt. You may choose to quilt in-the-ditch, echo the pieced or stamped motifs, use patterns from quilting design books and stencils, or do your own free-motion quilting.

BINDING

1. Trim excess batting and backing from the quilt.

2. Piece the binding strips together with diagonal seams to make a continuous binding strip.

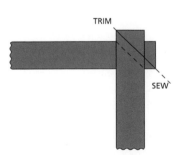

Overlap binding strips right sides together, stitch diagonally from notch to notch.

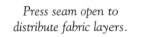

Press seam open to distribute fabric layers.

3. Press the seams open, then press the entire strip in half lengthwise with wrong sides together.

4. With raw edges even, pin the binding to the edge of the quilt a few inches away from the corner, and leave the first few inches of the binding unattached. Start sewing, using a 1/4" seam allowance.

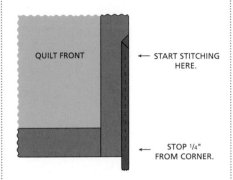

5. Stop 1/4" away from the first corner and backstitch. Remove the quilt from the sewing machine.

6. Fold the binding at a right angle so it extends straight above the quilt. Then bring the binding strip down even with the edge of the quilt.

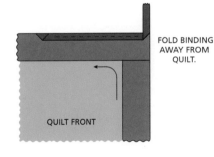

TURN COUNTERCLOCKWISE.

7. Begin sewing at the folded edge. Repeat in the same manner at all corners.

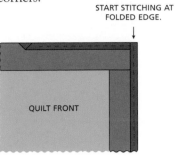

8. Finish off the binding by folding one end under 1/4" and overlapping it with the second end, trimming any leftover binding.

9. Fold the binding over the raw edge to the back of the quilt and blind stitch the binding to the back.

REFERENCES/PUBLICATIONS

BOOKS

Creating with Paint, Kahn, Sherrill, Martingale & Co., 2001, Bothell, WA.

Imagery on Fabric, Laury, Jean Ray, C&T Publishing, Inc., 1997, Lafayette, CA.

Nature Printing with Herbs, Fruits, and Flowers, Bethmann, Laura Donnelly, Storey Communications, Inc., 1996, Pownal, VT.

The Photo Transfer Handbook, Laury, Jean Ray, C&T Publishing, Inc., 1999, Lafayette, CA.

Print Your Own Fabric, Widger, Katy J., self-published, 2001, P.O. Box 2757, Edgewood, NM.

Rubber Stamps and How to Make Them, Thomson, George L. Pantheon Books, 1982, NY, NY.

Start Quilting with Alex Anderson, 2nd Edition, Anderson, Alex, C&T Publishing, Inc., 2002, Lafayette, CA.

PERIODICALS

Belle Armoire, 22992 Mill Creek, Suite B, Laguna Hills, CA 92653, (877) 782-6737, www.stampington.com.

Somerset Studio, 22922 Mill Creek Rd., Suite B, Laguna Hills, CA 92653, (714) 380-7318, www.somersetstudio.com.

Rubberstampmadness, 408 SW Monroe, #210, Corvallis, OR 97339-0610, (541) 752-0075, www.rsmadness.com.

SOURCE LIST

1. Art Supply Store
2. Craft or Hobby Shop
3. Grocery Store
4. Hardware Store
5. Rubber Stamp Shop
6. Daniel Smith, (800) 426-6740, www.danielsmith.com
7. Dharma Trading Co., (800) 542-5227, www.dharmatrading.com
8. Dick Blick, (800) 447-8192, www.dickblick.com
9. Nasco Arts and Crafts, (800) 558-9595, email: www.enasco.com
10. Pearl Paint, (800) 221-6845, www.pearlpaint.com
11. PRO Chemical and Dye, (800) 228-9393,www.prochemical.com
12. Rupert, Gibbon and Spider, Inc., (800) 843-8293, www.jacquardproducts.com
13. Sax Art and Crafts, (800) 558-6696, Fax (800) 328-4729
14. Spittin' Image, email spittinimage@worldnet.att.net
15. Stamp 'N Stor Mounting System, www.sundayint.com

For a free book catalog:
C&T Publishing, Inc.
P.O. Box 1456
Lafayette, CA 94549
(800) 284-1114
e-mail: ctinfo@ctpub.com
website: www.ctpub.com

For quilting supplies:
Cotton Patch Mail Order
3405 Hall Lane, Dept. CTB
Lafayette, CA 94549
(800) 835-4418
(925) 283-7883
e-mail: quiltusa@yahoo.com
website: www.quiltusa.com

STAMPING RESOURCES

Please check with your local stamping store first.

Acey Deucy
Check with your local stamping store.

All Night Media (owned by Plaid)

A.N.T. Transfer

Alice in Rubberland
(800) 842-4197
www.allnightmedia.com

Angel Stamp List
www.litlebit.com/angellist/sngellistpolicyonly.htm
www.rubberstampinglinks.com/angel-companies.html

Assyrian Guy
100 Proof Press
www.100proofpress.com

Asya Graphics
Check with your local stamping store.

Azadi Stamp Designs
www.limitededitionrs.com/azadi_stamp_design.html

Bizzaro
(401) 231-8777
www.bizzaro.com

CHUNKY STAMPS by Staoffengerg
Check with your local stamping store.

Co-Motion
Check with your local stamping store.

Columbia-Sign and Chart Printers
Check with your local stamping store.

Crazy Folk
Check with your local stamping store.

Daneland for Rubberland
Check with your local stamping store.

Rubber Stampede by Delta Disney
(800) 423-4135
www.deltacrafts.com/RubberStampede

Educational Insights
(800) 995-4436
www.edin.com

Effie Gletzfinger
Check with your local stamping store.

Emerald City Stamps
www.accessone.com

ERA Graphics
(408) 364-1124
www.ERAgraphics.com

Good Stamps-Stamp Goods
(800) 637-6401
www.rubberstampgoods,com

Granny Moon
Check with your local stamping store.

Graven Images
Check with your local stamping store.

Gumball Graphics
Check with your local stamping store.

The Happy Stamper
(303) 322-2489

The Happy Stamps
Check with your local stamping store.

The Herbarium
Sac'o 2-90-94

Hero Arts
(800) 822-HERO
www.heroarts.com

Impress Me
Sherrill Kahn
(818) 788-6730
www.impressmenow.com

Imprints Graphic Studio Inc.
(905) 660-5238
www.graphistamp.com

Inkadinkadoo
(800) 888-4652
www.inkadinkado.com

Kidstamps
Beatrix Potter
Fredric Warne & Co.

Judy-Kins
(310) 515-1115

Leavenworth Jackson
www.ljackson.com

Museum of Modern Rubber
(865) 584-9991
www.modernrubber.com

Neato Stuff
(888) PopOuts
www.popouts.com

100 Proof Press
(740) 594-2315
www.100proofpress.com

PSX Personal Stamp Exchang
(800) STAMP-IT
www.psxstamps.com

Plaid Enterprise, Inc.
Stamps for Kids
Simply Stamps
(800) 842-4197
www.allnightmedia.com

Polperro
Check with your local stamping store

Posh Impressions
(800) 421-7674
www.poshimpressions.com

Purrfection
Pelles
(800) 691-4293
www.purrfection.com

Quarter Moon
Check with your local stamping store

Raw Stamps
Check with your local stamping store

Red Pearl
Check with your local stamping store

Rubber Baby Buggy Bumpers
(970) 224-3499
www.rubberbaby.com

Rubber Stampede
(800) 632-8386

Rubber Stamp Works
Check with your local stamping store.

Rubber Stamps of America
Circus Stamps
(800) 553-5031
www.stampusa.com

Stampa Rosa Co.
(800) 554-5755
www.stamparosa.com

Stamp Affair
(800) 4-INKPAD
www.stampaffair.com

Stamp Crazy
Check with your local stamping store.

Stamp Francisco
Fruit Basket Upset
Ivory Coast Trading Poste
(415) 566-1018
www.stampfrancisco.com

The Stamp Man
(727) 363-8142
www.stampman.net

Stampa Barbara
www.stampabarbara.com

Stamp in the Hand Co.
(310) 329-8555
www.astampinthehand.com

Stampers Anonymous
(440) 333-7941
www.stampersanonymous.com

Stamps by Columbia
Check with your local stamping store.

Standard Rubber Type Co., Ltd
Check with your local stamping store.

Superior's Print Craft
Check with your local stamping store.

Susan Longerse
Check with your local stamping store.

Widger Stamps
Katy Widger
(505) 281-6174
www.katyjanewidger.com

Zeitology
Check with your local stamping store.

INDEX

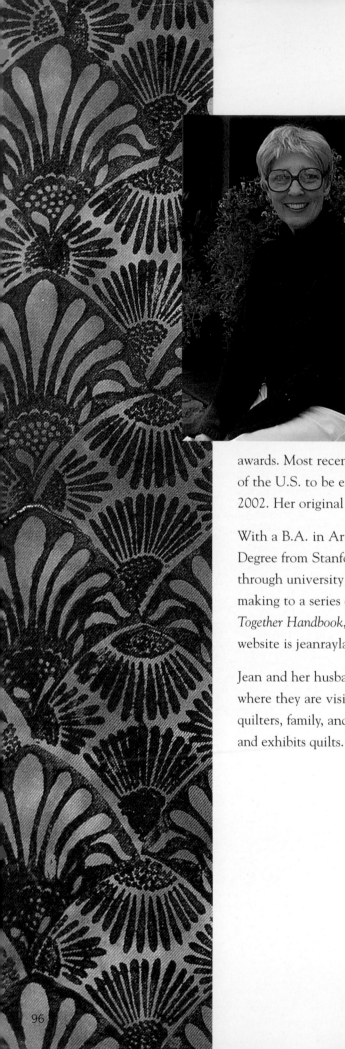

ABOUT THE AUTHOR

Jean Ray Laury is an exhibiting artist, writer, lecturer, and workshop teacher. Her interest in surface design is evident in her previous books, *Imagery on Fabric* and *The Photo Transfer Handbook*. This new book offers the same clarity, enthusiasm, and humor. Her ability to simplify and clarify all techniques makes her a popular teacher and a favorite source of information.

Jean has exhibited widely and received numerous awards. Most recently, she was selected as one of Thirty Distinguished Quiltmakers of the U.S. to be exhibited in the Tokyo International Great Quilt Festival in 2002. Her original quilts, often political, are non-conventional and humorous.

With a B.A. in Art and English from the University of North Iowa, and a Master's Degree from Stanford, she was well prepared for teaching (from junior high school through university). Her writing includes books ranging from quiltmaking and doll making to a series of satires, a children's book, *The Creative Woman's Getting-It-All-Together Handbook*, and *Ho for California: California Women and Their Quilts*. Her website is jeanraylaury.com.

Jean and her husband Frank, a retired professor of art, live in the Sierra foothills where they are visited regularly by wild turkeys, deer, foxes, grandchildren, quilters, family, and friends. She writes, gardens a little, reads a lot, and makes and exhibits quilts.